The Key is the Next Step: Moving from Salvation into the Kingdom of God

Francois Ahimou PhD

ISBN: 1-4565-7963-0
ISBN-13: 9781456579630

Dedication

I wish to dedicate this book to my wife, Anne, who is my life partner and my best friend, to my daughter Hannah-Grace, and to the many Pastors and Ministers around the world who are pouring out their lives for the sake of the Kingdom of God. Also, great thanks for the prayers and support from the Heaven Citizenship family. Special thanks must go to Tracie DeVine for her voluntary help with editing and arranging the book.

Contents

INTRODUCTION

One morning while driving with my wife, we were listening to a Christian radio station. A woman called in and shared a testimony about her mother's hospitalization. The woman was glad to see her mother's health condition improve from critical to stable, even though the state of illness was still serious. This exchange with the radio host caught my attention. I recall the woman saying, *"We are not going to complain because my mother is still alive. Praise the Lord!"* My perception was different. The woman's statement resounded in my heart, and I heard the Holy Spirit saying to me, *"One thing is to be alive, another is to be in good health"*. She was glad to see some improvement, and I was upset to see the devil still having a grip on her mother's life. Gladness and sickness can not fellowship together.

After arriving home, I prayed for the mother's complete healing and full restoration. While praying, God asked me to write a book about the difference between living in Victory and the state of being saved. Salvation refers to being alive; Victory refers to being in good health. People in the hospital are not free in their movement or action, even though they are alive. They are restricted to the hospital room, hallway, lobby, and surgery rooms, if needed.

God's goal is for His children to walk in Victory, not just to be saved. Salvation is the first step toward a successful and Victorious spiritual life in the Kingdom of God. God's goal is for His children to enjoy the fruit of the land.

Difference between *Kingdom of God and Heaven*

There are two main kinds of kingdoms on earth, the Kingdom of God and the kingdom of the devil, which is also called the "world". The earth and the "world" are different. The earth has been created by God, as explained in Genesis 2:4-7. Later in Revelation 12:7-9, the devil was cast out of Heaven onto earth. The devil introduced the "world" system with all its failure and corruption.

According to Mark 9:1, the Kingdom of God has a spiritual and physical existence. This is why Jesus said, "Assuredly, I say to you that there are some standing here who will not taste death till they see the kingdom of God present with power".

Seeing the Kingdom of God without experiencing physical death means the Kingdom of God is not in Heaven. Based on Mark 9:1, we understand that God intends for us to experience His Kingdom while on earth. The Kingdom of God and its benefits are located here on earth, as opposed to the benefits of Salvation which will occur in Heaven.

Importance of the Kingdom of God

The Kingdom of God finds its importance as the key message preached by Jesus. There are two main reasons that Jesus came, died, and paid the price for us. First, Jesus saved us through His crucifixion and resurrection. Second, Jesus established the Kingdom of God through His teaching and the manifestation of the Holy Spirit.

Jesus spent His whole Ministry preaching about the Kingdom of God. After He died and was resurrected, Jesus spent forty days preaching about how to live and demonstrate the Kingdom of God (Acts 1:3). He sent His disciples with instructions to preach this same message of the Kingdom of God (Luke 9:1-2).

The Kingdom of God has always been a priority. Jesus declared, "But seek first the kingdom of God and His righteousness, and all these things shall be added to you" (Matthew 6:33). Jesus persisted in preaching the message of the Kingdom of God. The crowd was so captivated that they tried to keep Him from leaving. Jesus responded by saying, "I must preach the kingdom of God to the other cities also, because for this purpose I have been sent" (Luke 4:42-43).

In John 10:40-41, the Bible says that John the Baptist did not perform any miracle beyond the Jordan River. This is where he conducted baptisms. Jesus went into this same region and changed the whole dynamic.

> "And He [Jesus] went away again beyond the Jordan to the place where John was baptizing at first, and there He stayed. Then many came to Him and said, 'John performed no sign, but all the things that John spoke about this Man were true'".

Jesus demonstrated the Kingdom of God in power. As Apostle Paul said, "The kingdom of God is not in word but in power" (1 Corinthians 4:20).

In other words, the Kingdom of God is always accompanied by action. Salvation itself does not move mountains out of a person's life. Taking action and using the Holy Spirit will move mountains. We must function as Victorious Christians.

Only the message of the Kingdom of God can bring revival in a person's life. Revival broke out in the early Church because the Kingdom of God was preached. The message of the Kingdom activates in people a pressing forward to know and experience freedom, peace, and joy.

Kingdom of God: Definition and Location

It is important to highlight that the Kingdom of God and the Kingdom of Heaven have the same meaning. The "Kingdom of Heaven" is used only in the book of Matthew, whereas the "Kingdom of God" is used throughout the New Testament. Matthew prefers the term "Kingdom of Heaven", due to his rabbinical, Jewish background which traditionally does not speak the name of God. Throughout this book, we will use the most common phrase, which is the Kingdom of God.

The Kingdom of God can be defined according to *Romans 14:17*. In this reference, the Bible says that *"The kingdom of God is not a matter of getting the food and drink, but instead it is about righteousness, peace, and joy in the realm of the Holy Spirit"*. In other words, to have access to the Kingdom of God, you must have a different priority than eating and drinking.

The characteristics of righteousness, peace, and joy in the Kingdom of God are distinct. These will be explained further in Chapter 5, yet briefly here.

Righteousness means right standing with God, with humans, and with God's commandments. Peace is not from the *"world"* and is not equivalent to lack of war. In *John 14:27*, Jesus says,

> *"Peace I leave with you, My peace I give to you; not as the world gives do I give to you. Let not your heart be troubled, neither let it be afraid".*

Then, the joy experienced in the Kingdom of God leads a person to continually rejoice *(Philippians 4:4)*.

Accessibility to the Kingdom of God

The Kingdom of God is accessible only to people who are already saved. The conversation between Jesus and Nicodemus teaches us of the necessity of being born again before entering the Kingdom of God.

> *"There was a man of the Pharisees named Nicodemus, a ruler of the Jews. This man came to Jesus by night and said to Him, 'Rabbi, we know that You are a teacher come from God; for no one can do these signs that You do unless God is with him.' Jesus answered and said to him, 'Most assuredly, I say to you, unless one is born again, he cannot see the kingdom of God.' Nicodemus said to Him, 'How can a man be born when he is old? Can he enter a second time into his mother's womb and be born?' Jesus answered, 'Most assuredly, I say to you, unless one*

*is born of water and the Spirit, he cannot enter the king-
dom of God'". (Luke 3:1-5)*

Jesus' response to Nicodemus in the previous reference
explains why Jesus revealed secrets of the Kingdom to His disciples, whereas He spoke in parables to those who were reject-
ing Him.

*"Then His disciples asked Him, saying, 'What does this
parable mean?' And He said, 'To you it has been given to
know the mysteries of the kingdom of God, but to the rest
it is given in parables, that 'Seeing they may not see, and
hearing they may not understand.' 'Now the parable is
this: The seed is the word of God'". (Luke 8:9-11)*

In other words, the priority for the others was not to get
into the Kingdom of God, but first to accept Jesus. You have
to accept Jesus Christ as your Savior before getting into the
Kingdom of God. Therefore, the Kingdom of God is for mature
Christians.

The Key: Spiritual meaning

The possession of the keys of the Kingdom of God enables
a person to reproduce the attributes of Heaven here on earth.
This is highlighted in *Matthew 16:19,* in The Amplified Bible.

*"I will give you the keys of the kingdom of heaven; and
whatever you bind (declare to be improper and unlaw-
ful) on earth must be what is already bound in heaven;
and whatever you loose (declare lawful) on earth must
be what is already loosed in heaven".*

The authority represented by the key needs to be fully understood and used by the Body of Christ. We have inherited
the Victory of Jesus over the devil. This was obtained in Heaven
and is given to us.

*"And war broke out in heaven: Michael and his angels
fought with the dragon; and the dragon and his angels
fought, but they did not prevail, nor was a place found*

for them in heaven any longer. So the great dragon was cast out, that serpent of old, called the Devil and Satan, who deceives the whole world; he was cast to the earth, and his angels were cast out with him". (Revelation 12:7-9)

We are called and must walk in Victory over all evil, which implies functioning in the Kingdom of God on earth.

Urgency of the Situation

Recently, many Christian books, conferences, and television shows have been organized around the topic of the Kingdom of God. The circumstances are urgent. People are realizing that it takes more than the state of just being saved.

The devil is much more impressed and intimidated by a person saved living in Victory than someone being just saved. For example, if a person tells you he is saved, you may not be surprised. However, if a person tells you he does not worry but rather lives in peace and joy all the time, this would be more striking because it is less common in this world.

Salvation is for Heaven, where the devil already lost the battle *(Revelation 12:9-10)*, whereas Victory is for the earth, where the battle is still going on. Many Christians have stopped at the first level, which is Salvation, instead of moving into Victory. The devil is always hiding knowledge. This is why God says, *"My people are destroyed for lack of knowledge"* (Hosea 4:6). Knowledge of the Word of God reveals your right.

In the 1970's in Ivory Coast (West Africa), where I was born and grew up, we experienced a series of outdoor crusades organized by the evangelical movement. The crusades resulted in many miracles, healings, signs, and wonders in different locations. I remember people with all kinds of infirmities being transported from villages to towns in order to receive healing through those powerful crusades. Testimonies were broadcast on radio and television, and led to churches being planted. Although healed of sickness, most people were still living in sin due to lack of knowledge. As a result, the devil came to possess them again, and many people that had been healed became sick again. One thing is to receive healing, and another thing is to keep that blessing. Righteousness helps you to keep God's blessing.

Spiritual healing helps God's people to maintain physical healing. The spiritual realm works ahead of the human realm. For example, when Jesus walked with a blind man outside the town, he perceived other men like trees, and then he received physical healing (Mark 8:22-25). The man's spiritual sight was restored first, and then he received physical sight. Similarly, Jesus taught us to first believe the response to prayer is granted, and then it will be seen (Mark 11:24). Jesus told us to seek first the Kingdom of God and righteousness, and then all else will be added. This is like the steps of a snow plow, where first snow is removed and then salt is spread to prevent freezing.

Knowledge about the Kingdom of God is necessary and vital today. This book will help you unfold the whole picture in order to understand that the main goal is to get into the Kingdom of God, and not just to be saved. The point is to finish the race, not just to start. The Bible says, "The end of a thing is better than its beginning..." (Ecclesiastes 7:8).

We have been saved to be used by God in His Kingdom. You can only be efficient in this battle against the devil if you live in Victory. Christians have been called and saved to bear fruit, which comes through righteousness, peace, and joy. When reading this book, here are a few questions for all to answer:

- · How long have you been Christian?
- · Do you consider yourself a Victorious Christian?
- · Are you someone who worries or is depressed?
- · What do you have to learn about the Kingdom of God?
- · What input should you bring to get into the Kingdom of God?

Answers to these questions will be discussed in the following chapters.

Furthermore, I often ask another key question to understand a person's spiritual level when assisting or praying for him/her: *"Can you identify a major turning point in your spiritual life?"* If the response to this question is unclear or no, this reveals that he/she is still at the Salvation step, not yet having moved into the Kingdom of God.

This book will help and teach you how to move from Salvation into the Kingdom of God through your Victorious spiritual life. You will learn about the five different steps that God has designed for you to experience in order to fulfill His promises for your life.

Chapter 1
SEED DEVELOPMENT CYCLE

You may be asking, *"How to move from Salvation into the Kingdom of God?"* Before I discuss this topic with you, it is important to present some basic concepts. This chapter will help you understand the main topic. The seed development cycle, which begins in the ground and comprises five different steps, will be used as an illustration.

- · Seed
- · Roots
- · Tree
- · Fruit
- · Second generation seed

Ground

The ground supports the seed development cycle. God created us by using the dust of the ground. The Bible is clear about the origin of human kind.

> *"This is the history of the heavens and the earth when they were created, in the day that the LORD God made the earth and the heavens, before any plant of the field was in the earth and before any herb of the field had grown. For the LORD God had not caused it to rain on the earth, and there was no man to till the ground; but a mist went up from the earth and watered the whole face of the ground. And the LORD God formed man of the dust of the ground, and breathed into his nostrils the breath of life; and man became a living being". (Genesis 2:4-7)*

Based on this Scripture, we have the same origin and pattern as the ground. The only difference is that we have God's Spirit, which gives us life. In contrast, the ground is inert. Human kind became a living being after God breathed into the nostrils of Adam.

The ground carries and creates wealth. Many resources, such as oil and minerals (diamonds, silver, gold, etc.) are in the ground. When God made us, He did not remove silver and gold, and just select the sand. The sample that God used to make human kind is a sample that has everything in it. This explains why every human being has been created to be prosperous and blessed. We are born and created to carry God's blessing. The first time God spoke to human kind (Adam and Eve), God commanded them to be fruitful, multiply, and fill the earth.

> "Then God said, 'Let Us make man in Our image, according to Our likeness; let them have dominion over the fish of the sea, over the birds of the air, and over the cattle, over all the earth and over every creeping thing that creeps on the earth.' So God created man in His own image; in the image of God He created him; male and female He created them. Then God blessed them, and God said to them, 'Be fruitful and multiply; fill the earth and subdue it; have dominion over the fish of the sea, over the birds of the air, and over every living thing that moves on the earth'". (Genesis 1:26-28)

In this principle of filling the earth, land plays a key role. Land should always be important for Christians. The more land you have, the more obedient and blessed you are in the fulfillment of God's command.

As noted in the Introduction, the "earth" and the "world" are different. God created the earth and everything in it. The world belongs to the devil. This is why Jesus said, "Do not love the world or the things in the world. If anyone loves the world, the love of the Father is not in him". (1 John 2:15)

The world system is about everything except God. It is a system put in place by the devil. The world system operates in the air, as referred to in the following Scripture.

"And you He made alive, who were dead in trespasses and sins, in which you once walked according to the course of this world, according to the prince of the power of the air, the spirit who now works in the sons of disobedience" (Ephesians 2:1-2).

Seed

A seed always has to be put in the ground to germinate. Everything that is required for germination is in the seed. The seed's response is related to the ground and the environmental conditions of water, oxygen, temperature and light. As you can see, a seed has to team up with the ground in order to germinate.

Seed germination is the process by which a seed develops into a seedling. Three fundamental conditions must exist before germination can occur.

- · The seed must be viable,
- · Dormancy conditions (which prevent germination) must be overcome, and
- · Proper environmental requirements must be met.

The next phase of the tree's growth is the emergence of the seedling above the soil surface. This is called seedling establishment. God starts everything He does in seed form. This spiritual law is established by God in *Genesis 1:11.*

"Then God said, 'Let the earth bring forth grass, the herb that yields seed, and the fruit tree that yields fruit according to its kind, whose seed is in itself, on the earth'; and it was so".

In other words, *"A seed producing a tree yields fruit with seeds in it".* Jesus is the Seed that has life in Him. Through His crucifixion and burial, the sowing process took place. Germination requires the input from the seed as well as from the ground. Similarly, the Salvation process requires input from Jesus and our willingness.

When Jesus said on the cross, *"It is finished"* (John 19:30), this implied that all viability and environmental conditions for seed germination have been met.

Roots

Roots are the result of the interaction between the seed and the ground. The ground has to make room for the roots to grow out of the seed. Good environmental conditions enable faster development.

Roots have two main roles. One is to take the nutrients from the ground and bring them to the tree. The second is to make the tree stable. So, a tree grows in two directions. A tree grows above and below the ground. Tree growth and fructification are strongly dependent upon the quality of the soil, environmental conditions, and root depth, as mentioned above.

Just as root development draws upon environmental conditions, our spiritual growth depends on our willingness and availability. Our spiritual life needs three main elements for growth and stability. These elements can be considered like a tripod.

- Word of God
- Prayer
- Fasting

The Word of God is the spiritual equivalent to food required by our body. In the same way, prayer is the spiritual respiration necessary for our soul. Finally, fasting cleans and maintains our spiritual being. These three elements represent the digestive system (Word of God), respiratory system (prayer), and excretory system (fasting). All elements are vital for our spiritual health.

The impact and significance of prayer can be seen with the Pentecost outpouring of the Holy Spirit. Between the time of Jesus' resurrection and appearance to His disciples, the Believers were in the upper room praying.

> "Then they returned to Jerusalem from the mount called Olivet, which is near Jerusalem, a Sabbath day's journey. And when they had entered, they went up into the upper room where they were staying: Peter, James, John, and Andrew; Philip and Thomas; Bartholomew and Matthew; James the son of Alphaeus and Simon the Zealot; and Judas the son of James. These all continued with one accord in prayer and supplication, with the women and Mary the mother of Jesus, and with His brothers". (Acts 1:12-14)

The disciples prayed continuously until being filled with the Holy Spirit. Their prayer enabled them to move from Salvation into the baptism of the Holy Spirit. Prayer creates the condition for the indwelling of the Holy Spirit, as water creates the condition for seed germination in the ground and sustains the development of the seed into a tree.

Tree

A tree develops both above and below the ground surface. Trees grow branches upward and outward. New leaves appear, as well as flowers in some cases. Trees that receive proper nutrients through roots can grow to their full height and maturity.

Trees are important in natural landscape because they prevent erosion and protect ecosystems with foliage. They also produce oxygen and reduce carbon dioxide in the atmosphere, as well as help to regulate ground temperatures. Trees are critical for life.

In speaking about our spiritual life, both tree roots and branches are essential. In other words, our roots in Jesus, represented by the process of being born again, will create stability and strength to overcome any trial or challenge. The upward, outward tree branch growth signifies the active presence and power of the Holy Spirit.

In the Bible, the strength of the Holy Spirit in God's people is represented by a tree. In *Isaiah 61:1-3*, we learn about the anointing of Jesus on His people planted as *"Trees of righteousness"*.

"The Spirit of the Lord GOD is upon Me, because the LORD has anointed Me to preach good tidings to the poor; He has sent Me to heal the brokenhearted, to proclaim liberty to the captives, and the opening of the prison to those who are bound; to proclaim the acceptable year of the LORD, and the day of vengeance of our God; to comfort all who mourn, to console those who mourn in Zion, to give them beauty for ashes, the oil of joy for mourning, the garment of praise for the spirit of heaviness; that they may be called trees of righteousness, the planting of the LORD, that He may be glorified".

Furthermore, we learn in *Psalm 1:1-3* that dwelling in the Word of God, which creates an atmosphere for the Holy Spirit to move, causes us to *"be like a tree planted by the rivers of water".*

From the very beginning with Adam and Eve, God communicated to His people about the importance of trees, and planted the tree of life in the very center of the garden.

"And out of the ground the LORD God made every tree grow that is pleasant to the sight and good for food. The tree of life was also in the midst of the garden, and the tree of the knowledge of good and evil". (Genesis 2:9)

Today still, we have been equipped by the Holy Spirit to grow as a tree rooted in Jesus.

Fruit

Many plants, including trees, produce fruit to enclose and protect their seeds. These seeds will then need to spread out in order to grow more new plants. In other words, fruit contains the offspring for the next generation trees.

When seed from within a fruit falls on fertile ground, it grows up into another tree. The second generation life cycle of the fruit-bearing tree begins. When more fruit is produced, more seed becomes available. A greater number of seeds for the second generation will spread and develop more trees.

Similarly, the Holy Spirit needs to operate freely in a person in order for him/her to bear fruit. Apostle Paul spoke about the fruit of the Spirit in his letter to the Galatians.

> "But the fruit of the Spirit is love, joy, peace, longsuffering, kindness, goodness, faithfulness, gentleness, self-control. Against such there is no law". (Galatians 5:22-23)

The parallel between the Holy Spirit and a tree can be seen as both bear fruit. The above Scripture can be read as, "But the fruit of the 'Tree' is love, joy, peace..." In other words, Jesus' presence strongly in a person yields to the manifestation of the Holy Spirit. This stage of bearing fruit represents the Kingdom of God.

A study of Romans 14:17, which refers to the attributes of the Kingdom of God, and Galatians 5:22-23, which highlights the fruit of the Holy Spirit, reveals a similarity.

> "For the kingdom of God is not eating and drinking, but righteousness and peace and joy in the Holy Spirit" (Romans 14:17).

The Kingdom of God is the manifestation of the fruit of the Holy Spirit. To enter the Kingdom of God, you have to first be saved, then born again, and also baptized in the Holy Spirit. It is important to note that our willingness to let the Holy Spirit operate through us relates to the production of fruit. The process for bearing fruit can be quenched by our sin. This is conveyed in the Scripture below.

> "And do not grieve the Holy Spirit of God, by whom you were sealed for the day of redemption. Let all bitterness, wrath, anger, clamor, and evil speaking be put away from you, with all malice. And be kind to one another, tenderhearted, forgiving one another, even as God in Christ forgave you". (Ephesians 4:30-32)

Second generation seeds and spreading

The second generation seed comes from within the first generation fruit. The second generation seed looks the same as the previously sown first generation seed. This second generation seed is intended to spread, trigger the next germination cycle, and occupy another land.

The similarity between the first and second generation seed is originally explained in *Genesis 1:11*.

> "Then God said, 'Let the earth bring forth grass, the herb that yields seed, and the fruit tree that yields fruit according to its kind, whose seed is in itself, on the earth'; and it was so".

This principle of seed multiplication is expanded upon in *Genesis 1:28*.

> "Then God blessed them, and God said to them, 'Be fruitful and multiply; fill the earth and subdue it; have dominion over the fish of the sea, over the birds of the air, and over every living thing that moves on the earth'".

The blessing released by God in *Genesis 1:28* is for the first, second, and each descending generation. The first cycle finds its fulfillment in the action of *"be fruitful and multiply"*. The second cycle finds its fulfillment in the process of *"fill the earth and subdue it; have dominion over...every living thing"*.

The Lord has commanded us to take dominion first over the fish of the sea, which represent blessing. This representation is illustrated in *Matthew 17:24-27*, when Jesus was asked about a tax payment. He told Peter to cast a hook, and a piece of money was found in the fish's mouth. Based on this Scripture, fish carry money, which represent blessing. When a person is living in the Kingdom of God, he commands blessings and does not lack. His reputation spreads at the city and regional level. For this reason, God commanded us to have spiritual dominion over the birds of the air, which represent principalities. It is important to note that the dominion starts with the fish first, before reaching the bird level. In other words, you cannot have dominion over a region if you are not blessed.

The second generation seed represents someone who has been through the steps of Salvation, the Baptism of the Holy Spirit, and the Kingdom of God. He/she is now ready to receive the mandate from the Lord to fulfill the assignment, which is to fill the earth and act on God's behalf. The assignment, in other words, is to be Jesus' ambassador on earth.

Interpretation of seed development cycle

The spiritual meaning of the different steps in the seed germination cycle and their corresponding major event are given in **Table 1**. These different steps are required to move from the beginning step of Salvation to the level of walking in daily Victory. This table will help you understand the following chapters in this book.

Table 1. Interpretation of Seed Development Cycle

Steps	Spiritual Meaning	Major Event
Ground	Human Kind	Creation
Seed	Jesus	Salvation
Roots	Willingness and Growth	Born Again
Tree	Holy Spirit	Baptism in the Holy Spirit
Fruit	Kingdom of God	Walking in Victory
Second Generation Seeds	Jesus' Ambassador on Earth	Mandate

We were made from the ground. Jesus, the Seed, was put in the ground for three days. Through His crucifixion, burial and resurrection, we have access to Salvation. Jesus' resurrection is represented by the seed germination process, and yields to the Holy Spirit, the tree. The rooting of the tree in the ground will enable the ground to bear fruit. In other words, the presence of the Holy Spirit in God's people enables us to bear fruit.

In the seed germination process, roots coming from the seed will crack the ground to enlarge it. Force is applied to make room in the ground. The power that enabled Jesus' resurrection on the third day is represented by the force applied by the seed on the ground in this germination process. The tomb was not able to hold Jesus and the devil was defeated. Through Jesus' resurrection, Salvation became accessible to all human kind.

To be born again, our willingness is necessary. Being born again involves breaking strongholds, if necessary, through deliverance. Jesus molds and shapes our life through the Holy Spirit. As we grow spiritually in prayer, the Word of God, and fasting, we yield the manifestation of fruit of the Holy Spirit. The fruit produced by the Holy Spirit has the second generation seed in it. This process creates the atmosphere which establishes the Kingdom of God and enables us to dwell in it.

In summary, Jesus is the first generation seed, and we are the second generation seed assigned to be spread in another location. The assignment is to be Jesus' ambassadors on earth.

In the following chapters, we are going to discuss the five different levels which will enable you to move from the beginning step of Salvation into the Kingdom of God.

- Salvation
- Born Again
- Holy Spirit
- Kingdom of God
- Mandate

Chapter 2
SALVATION

According to the Bible, God saved us by His grace through faith in Jesus. We can not take credit for what Jesus did. Salvation is not a reward for being good. Salvation is accessible to everyone, according to *Romans 10:13-14*.

> "For 'whoever calls on the name of the LORD shall be saved.' How then shall they call on Him in whom they have not believed?".

Salvation is symbolized by the Cross. Jesus paid the price, He carried the Cross, He died for us, and He gave His life for our sins so that we can be justified through Him. When a person repents, Jesus' blood is efficient to cleanse away all sins. Jesus forgives us, and does not hold us accountable for past sins. The Bible says in *1 John 1:9*,

> "If we confess our sins, he is faithful and just and will forgive us our sins and purify us from all unrighteousness".

Sin opens the door for the devil to get into a person's life. When a person remains committed to Jesus and keeps his/her back turned away from sin, the devil no longer has any legal right to operate in his/her life. When a person accepts Jesus as Savior, God writes his/her name in the Book of Life.

If you have not already accepted Jesus as your personal Savior, you have this awesome opportunity today. When you give your life to Jesus, His Blood is more than enough to redeem you. You will be given the opportunity to access Heaven. Salvation is the first step towards the Kingdom of God.

Definition

Through Salvation, we have access to Heaven. Heaven is the dwelling place of God. The physical location of Heaven is not on earth, but the attributes of Heaven—which are in the Kingdom of God—are manifested on earth. The Kingdom of God is the representation of Heaven on earth. The order of occurrence and location of Salvation and the Kingdom of God are not the same, as summarized in the following **Table 2**.

As shown in Table 2, the timing of entry and outcome for Salvation and the Kingdom of God are inverted. Salvation is for Heaven, whereas the Kingdom of God is for earth.

In regards to location, Jesus clarified that some people will see the Kingdom of God before dying *(Mark 9:1)*. So, the Kingdom of God is on earth. The state of being saved is opposed to the state of going to hell. The end results of being saved or being condemned to hell take place after physical death. On the contrary, the end results of dwelling in or out of the Kingdom of God happen on earth before physical death.

Table 2. Difference between Salvation and Kingdom of God

| | Order of Occurrence | | Location of Outcome |
	Entry	Outcome	Outcome
Salvation	First	After Death	In Heaven
Kingdom of God	Second	Before Death	On Earth

Score Two

Our assignment is to score two. This means we are Victorious in both locations, in Heaven (i.e., Salvation) and on earth (i.e., the Kingdom of God). If a person is saved yet struggling on earth, the devil has scored a point. However, a score of 2-0 means we are fulfilling the commandment to be fruitful, multiply, fill the earth, and take dominion. *(Genesis 1:28)*

When a person is in Heaven, he/she is happy because he/she is safe. When a person is in the Kingdom of God, he/she is happy because he/she is in Victory even while living on earth. Therefore, Salvation is for Heaven what Victory is for the Kingdom of God.

Original Purpose

God's ultimate goal for us has never been just Salvation. The first time God spoke to human kind, He was not referring to Salvation. Instead, God commanded human kind to be fruitful, to multiply, and to fill the earth.

When God created Adam and Eve and put them in the garden, they were both in God's presence. God did not refer to Salvation the first time He spoke to them. Before they sinned, they did not need Salvation. Salvation came after Adam and Eve failed. The purpose of Salvation is to solve the mistake of our forefathers.

The goal of the journey is not to be saved. The goal is to be blessed and to enjoy the fruit of the land. Salvation is very important, yet it is not the main goal. Once a person has received Salvation, the original goal stated in *Genesis 1:28* now has to be fulfilled.

Devil's Strategy

The devil always uses a *"strategy of stealing and yielding partially"*. By distracting Adam and Eve, he was trying to alter the goal of their journey. Still today, by hiding knowledge about the Kingdom of God, the devil is trying to mislead Christians from living the abundant and prosperous life that God intends. The devil tries to mislead Christians into being satisfied with little.

This is illustrated perfectly in *2 Kings 8:1-6*. In this Scripture, a woman's land was confiscated by the Philistines, who represent the devil. During the time of confiscation, the woman's land produced fruit, which represents blessing. By obtaining a favorable petition from the king, the land and all its fruit since the day of confiscation were restored, plus the interest generated. The woman obtained full restoration.

> *"Then Elisha spoke to the woman whose son he had restored to life, saying, 'Arise and go, you and your household, and stay wherever you can; for the LORD has called for a famine, and furthermore, it will come upon the land for seven years.' So the woman arose and did according to the saying of the man of God, and she went with her household and dwelt in the land of the Philistines seven years.*
>
> *It came to pass, at the end of seven years, that the woman returned from the land of the Philistines; and she went to make an appeal to the king for her house and for her land. Then the king talked with Gehazi, the servant of the man of God, saying, 'Tell me, please, all the great things Elisha has done'. Now it happened, as he was telling the king how he had restored the dead to life, that there was the woman whose son he had restored to life, appealing to the king for her house and for her land. And Gehazi said, 'My lord, O king, this is the woman, and this is her son whom Elisha restored to life.' And when the king asked the woman, she told him.*
>
> *So the king appointed a certain officer for her, saying, 'Restore all that was hers, and all the proceeds of the field from the day that she left the land until now'".* (2 Kings 8:1-6)

In this example, the devil was keeping the land and interest generated during the confiscation period. Two things were stolen, the land and the fruit generated during the occupation. The land can be interpreted as Salvation, and the fruit is the Kingdom of God. Both were originally stolen from human kind with Adam and Eve. The devil stole their benefits of being in God's presence and the fulfillment of God's blessing in their life.

Based on the devil's same *"strategy of stealing and yielding partially"*, he is hiding the Kingdom of God in order to just yield Salvation, which is not the goal of the journey. The devil is more intimidated by a person who is saved and living in the Kingdom of God, than a person who is just saved.

Jesus is aware of the devil's schemes. Jesus came to preach the Kingdom of God and focused on this message. Even after Jesus preached the Kingdom of God, still little is known about the topic in the Christian community today.

In reading this book, if you are not yet saved, God wants to give you Salvation and restore the original blessing that was released upon your life. If you are already saved, God's goal is to move you into the Kingdom of God, where you can enjoy the fruit of the land. The land belongs to our Father, and therefore it belongs to us.

In speaking about Salvation, it is important to recall the role of John the Baptist, as he introduced Jesus before His Ministry on earth. John the Baptist's main message was about repentance, the first step towards receiving Jesus as Savior.

> *"For I say to you, among those born of women there is not a greater prophet than John the Baptist; but he who is least in the kingdom of God is greater than he"* (John 7:28).

While John the Baptist brought many people to repentance and water Baptism, his message was not accompanied by miracles. When Jesus entered the same places as John the Baptist, Jesus changed the whole dynamic. Jesus Christ came to give you Victory experienced on earth. Likewise, it is important to note that Salvation itself is not enough for you to operate miracles. In order to be healed and to operate miracles on earth, you need to use the power of the Holy Spirit within you.

"And He [Jesus] went away again beyond the Jordan to the place where John was baptizing at first, and there He stayed. Then many came to Him [Jesus] and said, 'John performed no sign, but all the things that John spoke about this Man were true.' And many believed in Him there". (John 10:40-42—brackets added)

Without using the Holy Spirit, even when saved, you can not experience a Victorious Christian life. The Bible says in *Acts 20:35*, that *"It is more blessed to give than to receive"*. We have been called as a vessel for the advancement of God's Kingdom on earth. The Holy Spirit is the engine that creates the atmosphere of God's move on earth. This explains why a church without the Holy Spirit is dead.

God's Solution Strategy

Human wisdom recommends securing what you have before moving onto another step. This is like climbing a ladder. You make sure that you have a good footing before going up to the next step.

With God, *"The end of a thing is better than its beginning"* (*Ecclesiastes 7:8*), so He secures your end with Salvation first. God proceeds in this way because He has designed you to be a winner in both places, in Heaven and on earth. God is a winner and will never experience defeat.

God's strategy has always been to secure the end first. He is going to ensure your Salvation first, like a *"happy ending"* in movies. Then, God is going to work backwards to provide you Victory while on earth. By doing so, God shows that He cares first for your eternity in Heaven. The earth will pass away, while Heaven is eternal.

Another contrast between God's strategy and human wisdom is seen with Jesus' first miracle while at a wedding in Cana of Galilee. The taste of the wine that came from miraculously transformed water was better than the wine made by man. This amazed the master of the feast, who concluded, *"You have kept the good wine until now!"*

"Jesus said to them, 'Fill the waterpots with water.' And they filled them up to the brim. And He said to them, 'Draw some out now, and take it to the master of the feast.' And they took it. When the master of the feast had tasted the water that was made wine, and did not know where it came from (but the servants who had drawn the water knew), the master of the feast called the bridegroom. And he said to him, 'Every man at the beginning sets out the good wine, and when the guests have well drunk, then the inferior. You have kept the good wine until now!'" (John 2:7-10)

Just as Jesus showed His way is different than man's way, it is essential to know that Salvation, our end, is secured first. Then, God works backward to ensure our entry into the Kingdom of God in order to enable us to enjoy our transition on earth. Salvation is our first step toward the Kingdom of God.

Decision turned into action

After the decision to accept Jesus Christ, it is very important to connect with other Christians and go to Church. The Bible provides us examples of people who obtained Salvation and then followed Jesus. Bartimaeus was healed from physical and spiritual blindness, and then followed Jesus.

"Then Jesus said to him, 'Receive your sight; your faith has made you well.' And immediately he received his sight, and followed Him, glorifying God..." (Luke 18:42-43)

In another case, Peter and John prayed for healing of the lame man at the Gate called Beautiful. Right afterwards, the healed man went to worship and praise God, instead of going back home.

"So he, leaping up, stood and walked and entered the temple with them—walking, leaping, and praising God. And all the people saw him walking and praising God". (Acts 3:8-9)

Likewise, it is very important that our decision to follow Jesus turns into action. This implies attending Church, reading the Bible, praying, worshiping, and spending time in fasting.

We are saved by faith. The next step, being *"born again"*, requires our human input. This is a process that creates the atmosphere for the dwelling of the Holy Spirit in us.

Chapter 3
BORN AGAIN

According to the Bible *(Ephesians 2:8-9)*, our input in Salvation is not more than repenting and believing in Jesus. We are saved after making the decision to accept Jesus' death and resurrection, which grants us eternal life. The main part in the Salvation process is done by Jesus. We just have to add our belief to finalize the agreement. Receiving Salvation, however, does not mean that we are out of sin. We have made the decision to stop sinning, but this does not mean that our decision has already been turned into action.

There is a difference between Salvation and being *"born again"*. This difference is not always clearly understood in the Body of Christ. Salvation cleans and wipes your past from sin. This is a great shift in the spiritual realm. Salvation comes before being born again.

The process of being born again creates the conditions for new direction in your life. Being born again deepens our rooting in the Lord. Being born again involves major transformation, and is like a revolution, in our spiritual life. In the Bible, *2 Corinthians 5:17* highlights the importance of being born again. When a person is in grafted in Jesus Christ, he/she becomes a completely new creation, the old moral and spiritual condition is gone, and the fresh, new life has begun.

Behavior Speaks

We have all heard the question, *"How can a Christian behave like that?"* The answer is, *"Yes, a Christian can have such conduct if he/she is not born again"*. Before a person is born again, his/her behavior has not necessarily changed. Likewise, many people have been surprised by the carnal behavior of some Christians simply because they have not been born again.

Life experience shows that it takes time for a decision to be transformed into action. The next step will be a reflection of change in a person's conduct. One thing is to make a decision, and another is to apply it. Salvation is the decision, and being born again is the application.

Many Christians are saved, yet their life has not changed direction. Their behavior is not correlated to their decision. They have not been born again. Their testimony does not speak positively of Christianity. Their conduct is not promoting Jesus.

The American lecturer and essayist Ralph Waldo Emerson (May 25, 1803—April 27, 1882) said, *"Your actions speak so loudly that I cannot hear what you say"*. In other words, a person's actions have more impact than what he/she says. A person's actions tell more than what he/she claims through words.

In the same way, the unchanged behavior of a saved (not yet born again) Christian sends a mixed message. It is important for the changed behavior of Christians to be seen and heard. This will communicate a true and positive message about Jesus that draws unbelievers to Salvation. The conduct of born again Christians speaks boldly.

Changes Needed

One testimony related to actions speaking louder than words occurred during my experiences as a newly born again Christian in Ivory Coast (West Africa).

A Christian woman from the Church back in Africa shared that she was being persecuted by her husband. She claimed that he was against God and her attendance at Church. We prayed for her several times in order to break the spirit of persecution.

One day, our Pastor decided to visit this woman with some other Christians from the Church. Upon arriving at her home, we were surprised by a warm welcome from the husband. He offered us a place to sit and some water, based on our African culture.

Even before we presented our reason for visiting, the husband was curious to learn more about Jesus and explained the family situation. Based on his side of the story, the wife was persecuting him and characterized him as a "demon" in the house. The Pastor decided to further investigate the two different versions of this story. Someone was being persecuted, but who was the persecutor? Was it the husband or the wife?

According to their individual perspectives, the husband and wife were both right. For the unsaved husband, being Christian also implies being born again. For him, it did not make sense to attend Church if no sign of spiritual change occurred in a person's life. The wife's behavior is a perfect illustration of the difference between Salvation and being born again. She judged her husband as a demon and at the same time blamed him for lack of interest in becoming Christian. The wife's behavior did not open the door for her husband to attend Church, and he no longer saw any compelling reason to be saved. As a reaction, the husband was persecuting the wife.

The Pastor realized that both the husband and wife were in need of prayer. He met with them to provide counseling. The Pastor clearly presented the Gospel to the husband, providing another perspective than the wife's example. The husband was touched, decided to give his own life to Jesus and also became a member of the Church. Through this experience, the wife realized the importance of being born again and opening the door of Salvation for other family members.

As seen in this testimony, being born again is a critical step after Salvation. Your family members, friends, co-workers, and neighbors can only change if they see such change in you.

Sinful Nature

Through our inherited nature from Adam and Eve, we are all sinners. The *"default setting"* after Adam and Eve's failure is to sin. This demonstrates why it is easier to live in sin than righteousness; it is easier to make war than peace; and it is easier to hate than forgive. Our human nature is proud. For this reason, Jesus said that our flesh must be crucified. According to *Romans 6:6*, our *"old self"* was nailed to the Cross with Jesus so that sin no longer has the power to enslave us to evil. We are given the opportunity to be spiritually crucified with Jesus. In this way, we are qualified to live outside of sin, leading a righteous and holy life.

It is important to understand that sin opens doors to the devil, giving him a legal right to operate in a person's life. Sin makes a person a slave spiritually to the devil, as opposed to righteousness, which makes a person spiritually free. Righteousness and holiness draw a person close to God, as opposed to sin, which creates a distance between a person and God. The Bible is clear about the consequences of sin, as stated in the following Scripture.

> *"Behold, the LORD's hand is not shortened, that it cannot save; nor His ear heavy, that it cannot hear. But your iniquities have separated you from your God; and your sins have hidden His face from you, so that He will not hear".* (Isaiah 59:1-2)

Bloodlines

It is important to understand the effects of a bloodline, as well as how these effects are cancelled through giving your life to Jesus and being born again. A bloodline is a spiritual *"DNA"* resulting from a generational link inherited from the mother's or father's side. According to *Genesis 1:11*, we are a product of our parents.

> *"Then God said, 'Let the earth bring forth grass, the herb that yields seed, and the fruit tree that yields fruit according to its kind, whose seed is in itself, on the earth'; and it was so".*

A bloodline results in a generational, spiritual covenant. A bloodline has the ability to transfer the consequences of sins or curses from one generation to another generation.

Bloodlines through Inheritance

Abraham's Descendants

Abraham carried God's promise and blessing, which extended to his descendants Isaac, Jacob, and Joseph. At the same time, due to Abraham's sin with his wife's servant, Hagar, he introduced a sexual issue to the family. This bloodline of sexual perversion manifested in the life of his grandson, Jacob, who married two sisters, Leah and Rachel. This abnormality is seen as Leah and Rachel's children were at same time cousins and brothers. This is explained in *Genesis 29:26-30*.

> *"Laban replied, 'It is not our custom here to give the younger daughter in marriage before the older one. Finish this daughter's bridal week; then we will give you the younger one also, in return for another seven years of work.' And Jacob did so. He finished the week with Leah, and then Laban gave him his daughter Rachel to be his wife. Laban gave his servant Bilhah to his daughter Rachel as her attendant. Jacob made love to Rachel also, and his love for Rachel was greater than his love for Leah. And he worked for Laban another seven years".*

The first born from this sexual confusion, Reuben from the fourth generation, perpetuates the bloodline. He slept with the concubine of his father, Jacob, as noted in *Genesis 35:22*.

> "And it happened, when Israel dwelt in that land, that Reuben went and lay with Bilhah his father's concubine; and Israel heard about it".

Furthermore, after Joseph received revelation through two dreams that he was chosen by God to carry out Abraham's promise, the devil used this sexual weakness bloodline to tempt him. The devil tried to comprise his blessing. This occurred through Potiphar's wife, who presented herself to lay with Joseph. God closed the door, and Joseph Victoriously escaped the situation. This event is explained in *Genesis 39:7-12*.

> "And it came to pass after these things that his master's wife cast longing eyes on Joseph, and she said, 'Lie with me.' But he refused and said to his master's wife, 'Look, my master does not know what is with me in the house, and he has committed all that he has to my hand. There is no one greater in this house than I, nor has he kept back anything from me but you, because you are his wife. How then can I do this great wickedness, and sin against God?' So it was, as she spoke to Joseph day by day, that he did not heed her, to lie with her or to be with her. But it happened about this time, when Joseph went into the house to do his work, and none of the men of the house was inside, that she caught him by his garment, saying, 'Lie with me.' But he left his garment in her hand, and fled and ran outside".

David's Descendants

Another Biblical illustration of family bloodline is with David and his descendants. David committed adultery with Bathsheba, the wife of Uriah the Hittite. Bathsheba became pregnant and bore a son who died seven days after his birth. After the death of Uriah in the battle field, David married Bathsheba. Solomon is David's second son with Bathsheba. This account is seen in *2 Samuel 11:1-5*.

> *"In the spring, at the time when kings go off to war, David sent Joab out with the king's men and the whole Israelite army. They destroyed the Ammonites and besieged Rabbah. But David remained in Jerusalem. One evening David got up from his bed and walked around on the roof of the palace. From the roof he saw a woman bathing. The woman was very beautiful, and David sent someone to find out about her. The man said, 'She is Bathsheba, the daughter of Eliam and the wife of Uriah the Hittite.' Then David sent messengers to get her. She came to him, and he slept with her. (Now she was purifying herself from her monthly uncleanness.) Then she went back home. The woman conceived and sent word to David, saying, 'I am pregnant'".*

In this case, David and Bathsheba's adulterous relation created a generational bloodline. This bloodline was passed onto the descendants, and resulted in the well-known case of Solomon. The Bible clearly states that King Solomon *"Had seven hundred wives of royal birth and three hundred concubines, and his wives led him astray"* (1 Kings 11:3). We see how this adulterous bloodline was not only transferred to King Solomon, but also intensified its impact over generations.

Cain's Descendants

The variable manifestation of bloodlines can be seen through the descendants of Cain, the first son of Adam and Eve. Cain murdered his brother, Abel. Certain negative consequences of this sinful action remain dormant in the bloodline until popping up again in the sixth generation with Lamech. This is referenced in *Genesis 4:16-23*, and presented in **Table 3**.

In addition to the emergence of this murder bloodline with Lamech, a new bloodline called polygamy was also introduced. *"Polygamy"* is defined as having more than one spouse at one time. Bloodlines, if not spiritually cut, can develop throughout generations and yield to other kinds of bloodlines and consequences.

Table 3. Descendents of Cain

Generation	First-Born Name	Effect of Bloodline
1st	Cain	Murder (Genesis 4:8)
2nd	Enoch	—
3rd	Irad	—
4th	Mehujael	—
5th	Methushael	—
6th	Lamech	Murder (Genesis 4:23) Polygamy (Genesis 4:19)

Bloodlines through Marriage

In marriage, any sinful, inherited bloodlines with the man or woman—if not already delivered—will be incorporated. The unified man and woman come from input on both sides. A bloodline can develop into a stronghold. Two spirits merge into one spirit, as explained in *Genesis 2:24*.

"Therefore a man shall leave his father and mother and be joined to his wife, and they shall become one flesh".

It is important to know whom you are marrying and what the family pattern looks like, and if needed, go through deliverance first before getting married. The husband, wife, and descendants will be impacted, either positively or negatively, in regards to conduct and spiritual position.

Today, many people do not take time to ask God about His will before getting married. Christians today can not wait. Material and financial interests are nowadays motivating people to get married. The world is impacting the Church, instead of the Church impacting the world.

Freedom from Negative Bloodlines

Spiritual Check-up

A person can experience struggles related to a bloodline, even though his direct parents did not. It is necessary to check back through many generations of a family, even if the present generation seems fine. Bloodlines can be hidden if not revealed.

For example, the bloodline introduced through Abraham's adulterous relation with his wife's servant, Hagar, was hidden during Isaac's generation, but then popped up with his grandson, Jacob. Sins resulting from bloodlines do not necessarily appear in every consecutive generation.

It is very important for every Christian to go through a spiritual scanning process after receiving Salvation. This will identify and close any door that may be open to the devil due to sinful, generational bloodlines. Each generation has the capacity to break the cycle of sin and bloodlines. As Jesus said on the Cross, *"It is finished"* (John 19:30).

When a bloodline is not cut and continues through several generations of a family, its impact is extended in particular ways. At the individual level, a bloodline can corrupt a person's mind and expectations such that certain limitations and weaknesses seem completely normal and fine. This results in self-underestimation.

The negative effects of a bloodline are not limited to individual and family levels. Bloodlines can reach the tribal, country, and continental levels. This development depends on factors including family size, spiritual atmosphere, number of generations, and duration.

Case of Gideon

The case of Gideon is a perfect illustration of the effects of a negative bloodline. Gideon's thoughts had been corrupted, resulting in low esteem of self and family. He was speaking a different language than God. Gideon was depending on his own strength and family history, while God asked him to trust in God's strength. Gideon was insisting on following his former ways (which were the family bloodline), while God wanted to give him a new reputation.

Even so, God spoke to Gideon differently. God revealed the opportunity we now have through being born again and deliverance to overcome negative generational bloodlines. This is highlighted in the Scripture passage below.

> *"Then the LORD turned to him and said, 'Go in this might of yours, and you shall save Israel from the hand of the Midianites. Have I not sent you?' So he said to Him, 'O my Lord, how can I save Israel? Indeed my clan is the weakest in Manasseh, and I am the least in my father's house.'*

And the LORD said to him, 'Surely I will be with you, and you shall defeat the Midianites as one man'". (Judges 6:14-16)

Today, a lot of people have the same attitude as Gideon. They always see themselves according to their past, instead of seeing themselves according to their future. God always speaks the future, because this is the language that the devil can not understand. Just as historical data about our life is stored and accessible, the devil knows our past and present. However, when it comes to a Christian's future, the devil has no idea and can only guess.

Curses

Curses and blessings are both by default generational, unless intentionally broken. Prayer breaks generational curses in the way that sin cancels generational blessings.

A curse is a prayer for evil to fall upon a person or region. It is an invocation for misfortune, injury, or harm to come upon someone. A curse can be directly or indirectly released in a person's life. In the later case, spiritual discernment is necessary for a person to become aware of underlying or implied curses. The expression of an inherited curse or blessing is called a bloodline.

Individual Level

The recipient of a curse can be an individual person. A curse can be pronounced purposely, or without realizing the impact of words spoken. A curse is a spiritual arrow that must be broken as soon as identified.

A curse can be released from three different sources:

· From the recipient him/herself,
· From another individual, or
· From a group of people.

Confusion

Many people, including Christians, speak negatively and curse without even realizing they are limiting their own selves. What he/she is asking is not consistent with what he/she is saying. This is a perfect expression of confusion.

This spirit of confusion causes Christians to close the door to their blessing even before asking God to provide. The words released fight their own blessing and put them in a difficult position to receive from God. They ask God to fill them, but the impact of their words is creating the opposite effect at the same time. The Bible says that, *"If a house is divided against itself, that house cannot stand"* (Mark 3:25).

God's Language about your Future

You must speak God's language if you want God to understand you. God's language is positivity, hope, opportunity, and future. This reveals the importance of renewed thinking with a Kingdom of God mind-set. You need to enlarge your territory and capacity in order for God to fill you. Another illustration is how the emptiness of a gasoline tank allows it to be completely filled up.

In today's world, people always ask *"Where are you from?"* when meeting a new person. This obeys the principle of building on your past. This principle is reflected with *"background checks"* required for new jobs or bank loans. People make judgments according to a person's background.

No matter what you have been through or are currently experiencing, your future is greater than your past. God does not build your future on your past, as the devil does.

In contrast, what really matters for God is *"where you are going"* and *"your willingness to change"*. As the Bible says, *"The end of a thing is better than its beginning…"* (Ecclesiastes 7:8). God values your end point more than your past. God has the ability to probe and detect a person's willingness to change direction at a very early stage. God's judgment is based upon your willingness to change, whereas human judgment is based upon the completion of the change process. God always works in advance, whereas the human system works according to present and rational facts.

"Never let your past decide for your future". God always gives opportunity to a person who is willing to change. Our future has been designed by God to be greater than our past. This is illustrated in *Haggai 2:9*, as the Lord says, *"The glory of this latter temple shall be greater than the former"*.

The devil's Strategy

Previous disappointment and bad experiences can cause many people, including Christians, to become trapped. The devil works a demonic strategy at two levels. First, he creates issues in a person's life, such as domestic violence, sexual abuse, divorce, death of a loved one, or loss of a job. Second, the devil traps a person by putting his/her focus on past, misfortunate events.

As a result of this cycle, a person (outside the Kingdom of God) does not see the end of the tunnel. When confined in this trap, it can result in cursing oneself to the point of committing suicide. A curse leads to spiritual death, which can then lead to physical death. In other words, death can be the outcome of curses.

It is important to remember that God loves the world so much that He gave us His only Son *(John 3:16)*. Through Jesus' crucifixion and resurrection, we have Salvation. *"There is therefore now no condemnation to those who are in Christ Jesus, who do not walk according to the flesh, but according to the Spirit"* (Romans 8:1).

During my experience in Ministry, I have prayed for people close to divorce or suicide due to issues like those mentioned previously. God, in His Grace, has set them free. Today, some of these people are members of my Church.

Power of the Tongue

We know that God created the earth by His Word, which shows the significance of power in the tongue. We have been created in God's image with His Spirit in us, and therefore, every word released by our mouth is a seed. A seed when sown in the ground generates a tree that will later bear fruit, either good or bad. A seed sown bears fruit, just like words released by someone can impact a person's future.

The Bible highlights the importance of being attentive to what comes out of a person's mouth. At times, our first enemy is our own thoughts and what proceeds from our own mouth. No matter what a person may go through, the spirit of negativity needs to be fought.

> "Out of the same mouth proceed blessing and cursing" (James 3:10).

> "Not what goes into the mouth defiles a man; but what comes out of the mouth, this defiles a man" (Matthew 15:11).

You are what you say you are. God said, "'Let there be light'; and there was light" (Genesis 1:3). Everything that you pronounce has an impact in the spiritual realm. Similarly, Christians have been given distinct power and authority to impact our surroundings. This is referenced in *Luke 10:19* and *Matthew 16:19*.

> "Behold, I give you the authority to trample on serpents and scorpions, and over all the power of the enemy, and nothing shall by any means hurt you" (Luke 10:19).

> "I will give you the keys of the kingdom of heaven, and whatever you bind on earth will be bound in heaven, and whatever you loose on earth will be loosed in heaven" (Matthew 16:19).

Noah and Adam

The life of Noah and his three sons (Shem, Ham, and Japheth) illustrates the impact of words spoken upon an individual's life. The descendants of Ham were cursed because Ham saw his father's nakedness and failed to respond appropriately. In contrast, Shem and Japheth were blessed for using a garment to cover their father's nakedness, while respectfully turning their faces towards the east, which means God's glory. (Genesis 9:18-29)

Noah and Adam's life present an interesting parallel. At certain points, they both became aware of their own nakedness, which speaks about the removal of God's spiritual covering. Adam failed by food, and Noah by drink. Also, they both behaved as "local" people, even though God had commanded them to be fruitful, multiply, and fill the earth.

Regional Level

Individual and regional curses are interrelated. A curse can be released upon an entire region through a person. A regional curse can also impact an individual person. It goes both ways. Furthermore, the spiritual impact of a blessing can also spread across a region.

This concept of regional impact is illustrated by a Christian in the workplace. When God's financial blessing is released upon a Christian, his/her business department and company are also blessed. For a Christian to receive a promotion, the company's revenue has to support it. As a result, an entire company can be blessed because of one person.

From the time of creation, God has spoken about land. God pronounced His blessing on Adam and Eve in Genesis 1:28, which implied the ground was blessed in order to accommodate them. God gave Adam and Eve full control over the land, assigning them to be the earth's covering.

> "Be fruitful and multiply; fill the earth and subdue it; have dominion over the fish of the sea, over the birds of the air, and over every living thing that moves on the earth".

In this verse, God established a spiritual hierarchy. God was Adam and Eve's covering, and they in turn were the earth's covering. The blessing released upon Adam and Eve's life flowed to the earth.

Spiritual hierarchy

Spiritual hierarchy and covering is seen in Ministries today. The relationship between God and a minister impacts the whole congregation. In other words, a person's spiritual life is dependent upon his/her spiritual covering. It is important to pay attention to the covering under which a person places himself/herself.

When a covering is cursed, everything underneath it is cursed as well. Similarly, after Adam and Eve sinned and were cursed, the ground inherited the consequence of its covering *(Genesis 3:17)*. In other words, the ground was cursed, so anything coming from it could not have God's approval. This is one reason why Cain's offering to God was not approved, since it was fruit from the cursed ground *(Genesis 4:1-5)*.

Zoar

The meaning of a name associated to region can impact the reputation and future of that region and its people. Names can carry a curse or blessing. Recently, I discovered that my first name, *"Francois"*, comes from *"Francis"* (Latin) and means *"free man"*. This is a blessing.

In the Bible, we learn of the city *"Zoar"*, which means *"small"* or *"insignificance"* in Hebrew. This name carries a curse. Abraham's nephew, Lot, took refuge in Zoar after fleeing the destruction of Sodom and Gomorrah. Lot dwelled in Zoar, near the southeast end of the Dead Sea, with his two daughters. In the subsequent events in Lot's family, we see how the meaning of Zoar negatively impacted his future.

Lot relocated with his two daughters from Zoar to the mountains, and then to a cave. While dwelling in an underground cave, which symbolizes spiritual death, Lot's daughters gave him alcohol and slept with him to gain children. Lot became the father and grandfather of the resulting children, named Moab and Ben-Ammi. This is the origin of the Moabites and Ammonites.

The lineages of these children born out of incest carried a curse. The Moabite and Ammonite nations carried the legacy of Lot's sin with his daughters. The resulting impact of such curses can spread upon a region. *(Genesis 19:22-36)*

Moab

The unfortunate outcome of a regional curse is clearly seen with the Moabites, the lineage derived from Moab, the first-born son of Lot's incestuous relations. The meaning of Moab is *"Who is your father?"*

Elimelech moved to Moab with his wife, Naomi, and two sons. Elimelech relocated from Bethlehem, which means *"House of Bread"*, to Moab, which means *"Who is your father?"* The family entered a region cursed as a *"fatherless"* land. While in Moab, Elimelech, the father of the family, died. This is consistent with the curse of the region. Afterwards, both sons of Elimelech married women from Moab. The same *"Who is your father?"* regional curse fell upon these sons, and they died. After these events, Naomi decided to leave the Moab region that was killing men.

One Moabite widow, Ruth, decided to follow Naomi in returning to Bethlehem. This action reversed the trend from *"Who is your father?"* back to *"House of Bread"*. The spiritual meaning of bread is *"revelation"*.

As Ruth relocated, she moved from *"death"* to *"life"*. Ruth was remarried to Boaz, and kept this husband. The regional curse that had been upon Ruth was removed, and the family continued for generations. Jesus Christ comes from the family lineage with Boaz. *(Book of Ruth)*

Nazareth

Nazareth is the city where Jesus grew up as a child. Nazareth had a poor reputation and lacked success. Everyone from Nazareth was condemned to be under this curse and its consequence.

The reputation of Nazareth was evident in Nathaniel's question, "Can anything good come out of Nazareth?" (John 1:16). This comment reflects the regional reputation, and indirectly expresses a curse.

Nathaniel's posing of this question occurred before he knew Jesus. Of course, outside of Jesus, nothing good can come out of a region. Jesus came to break any curse, including this one from Nazareth where He grew up.

How to break curses

Jesus' blood is more than enough to break any individual or regional curse. In Jesus, we are free. The Bible says that, "No weapon formed against you shall prosper, and every tongue which rises against you in judgment you shall condemn" (Isaiah 54:17).

This is an overview of three main points involved in breaking curses off a person's life.

- Identify curses that can be introduced or hidden at your individual level and/or through your ancestors.
- Cancel any curses by prayer and, if needed, go through deliverance.
- See yourself as free from the curse(s) and speak according to Isaiah 43:18-19.

"Do not remember the former things, nor consider the things of old. Behold, I will do a new thing, now it shall spring forth; shall you not know it? I will even make a road in the wilderness and rivers in the desert".

Furthermore, once a person has gained knowledge about curses, it is important to remain spiritually attentive. In other words, it is important to react promptly when any other curse may be released.

This is an overview of how to react to curses.

· Rebuke and cancel the curse as soon as it is released.
· Be confident in the Lord and know who you are in Christ.
· Proclaim blessing over yourself and your family.
· Use discernment in responding to what people say about you.

Walking Boldly

In responding boldly to any curse, a Christian is taking action according to the Word of God. It is foundational to keep your eyes on what is coming, and no longer rely on your past. In 2 Corinthians 5:17, the Bible says, "If anyone is in Christ, he is a new creation; old things have passed away; behold, all things have become new".

In the example of Bartimaeus, we see how to overcome comments and curses from the crowd based on a person's past. When Jesus commanded this blind man to come forth, Bartimaeus boldy threw "Aside his garment, he rose and came to Jesus" and received his healing (Mark 10:50). The throwing away of the garment symbolizes the abandon of Bartimaeus' old nature, and the immediate embrace of a new journey with Jesus.

When we have made a decision like Bartimaeus—renouncing curses and embracing a new life in Jesus—we have no obligation to entertain other curses, blame, or negativity. The Bible says that, "There is now no condemnation to those who are in Christ Jesus, who do not walk according to the flesh, but according to the Spirit" (Romans 8:1).

In our relationship with Jesus, we are called to partner with Him like teamwork. Our business is to believe, and God's business is to bless us. We do not need to figure out how the blessing is going to come. Just believe and you shall see. We do not walk by sight, but by faith. Faith enables you to receive from God, and signs follow for a testimony. It is important to let God fulfill His promise in your life.

Deliverance

Critical Awareness

I have been praying for the *"deliverance"* of new believers and Christians for over twenty years on four continents (Africa, Europe, Asia, America). To God be all the glory! I have found that many people, including Christians, lack an awareness of bloodlines and curses. When aware, Christians often lack the necessary knowledge about how to be delivered. I have come to the conclusion that curse and stronghold inheritance from bloodlines is a topic that must be identified, understood, and overcome. Both acknowledging and dealing with bloodlines and curses is critical for an individual and his/her future generations.

It is important to teach people how to get out of negative, generational bloodlines. Bloodlines can result in issues such as rejection, sexual abuse and perversion, divorce, lack of marriage, children out of wedlock, anger, poverty, alcoholism, drug addiction, smoking, worry, anxiety, and others. When the devil has been allowed to freely operate from generation to generation, he converts a bloodline into a stronghold. In other words, family tree roots can develop under the ground of a bloodline curse, resulting in a stronghold.

Often times, Christians do not know how to deal with the origin of the issues in which they find themselves. As the Word of God says in *Hosea 4:6*, *"My people are destroyed for lack of knowledge..."* It is important to learn about how to be set free. It takes deliverance to break strongholds resulting from bloodlines. When deliverance is needed yet not completed, bloodlines can affect a person's life.

A person should not rush into deliverance, but rather pray for an efficient strategy to kick the devil out. In praying for deliverance, no demonic force or stronghold can resist the name of Jesus. The Bible says, in *Romans 8:31*, that *"...If God is for us, who can be against us?"* In Jesus' name, we are more than Victorious. The Bible also says in *Isaiah 54:17*, that,

> "'No weapon formed against you shall prosper, and every tongue which rises against you in judgment you shall condemn. This is the heritage of the servants of the LORD, and their righteousness is from Me,' says the LORD".

Getting into God's Kingdom

Deliverance from bloodline sins, curses, and strongholds must be completed before a person can enter the Kingdom of God. In other words, lack of deliverance prevents a person from getting into the Kingdom of God.

Deliverance is critical for the advancement of God's Kingdom. Jesus cast out demons, healed the sick, and preached the message of the Kingdom of God in villages and regions where He travelled. Through Jesus, we see the importance of deliverance. Likewise, Jesus sent His disciples with the authority to cast out demons, heal the sick, and preach the message of the Kingdom of God. This is highlighted in *Luke 9:1-2*.

> "Then He called His twelve disciples together and gave them power and authority over all demons, and to cure diseases. He sent them to preach the kingdom of God and to heal the sick".

Note that in this Scripture, the topics are not listed randomly. The order demonstrates Jesus' priority. First, demons must be cast out, next a person receives healing, and then the opportunity will be given to him/her to enter the Kingdom of God.

The order of these steps is reversed with Salvation. For example, a person must accept Jesus first, while believing that He is capable to deliver and heal him. The Bible is clear about the role of faith as we come to Jesus.

> "And without faith it is impossible to please God, because anyone who comes to him must believe that he exists and that he rewards those who earnestly seek him" (Hebrews 11:6; NIV).

As seen here, Salvation is the first step. A person needs to have accepted Salvation in order to receive and keep healing from God. A person needs to be delivered and healed before getting into the Kingdom of God. In other words, the Kingdom of God comes after the step of Salvation.

Deliverance is between Salvation and the Kingdom of God. Deliverance is the bridge that connects Salvation to being born again, which then leads to Baptism in the Holy Spirit and entry into the Kingdom of God.

Willingness to go through Deliverance

Being saved does not imply a person is automatically delivered from all spiritual bondage. Every new Christian must have his spiritual life reviewed in order to detect and determine if deliverance is needed. Some strongholds, such as addictions and generational curses, can be hidden from an individual as well as his/her spiritual leader. The Holy Spirit always reveals what is hidden. Through deliverance, the Holy Spirit always reveals more than expected. It is the responsibility of every leader in the Body of Christ to make sure every Christian is spiritually clean and free.

It is important not to rush into deliverance. Two conditions must be met.

- Make sure the person is willing to go through deliverance. God will never force a person to do something against his/her will.

- Make sure the person is not sent by the devil to the Church, operating under "spiritual camouflage". These people will always delay, waste time, as well as attempt to undermine the anointing and power given by God to the local Church leader.

Here are specific examples of how the devil can send people to a Church. The examples include Scripture and testimony.

In *Acts 16:16-18*, the Bible speaks of deliverance and "spiritual camouflage". In this passage, a slave girl working as a fortune teller continuously and loudly repeated a true fact about Apostle Paul and his disciples.

> "Now it happened, as we went to prayer, that a certain slave girl possessed with a spirit of divination met us, who brought her masters much profit by fortune-telling. This girl followed Paul and us, and cried out, saying, 'These men are the servants of the Most High God, who proclaim to us the way of salvation.' And this she did for many days. But Paul, greatly annoyed, turned and said to the spirit, 'I command you in the name of Jesus Christ to come out of her.' And he came out that very hour".

In this passage, the presented statement about God's servants is true, but the girl speaking was demon-possessed. The devil was using a strategy of "spiritual camouflage" and confusion. Apostle Paul, with revelation from the Holy Spirit, cast out these demons and set the girl free.

In *Luke 4:33-36*, a demon-possessed man felt comfortable in the synagogue until Jesus arrived. As soon as Jesus appeared, the man was the first to speak. The demons in him reacted and were afraid. Jesus cast out those demons and set the man free.

> "Now in the synagogue there was a man who had a spirit of an unclean demon. And he cried out with a loud voice, saying, 'Let us alone! What have we to do with You, Jesus of Nazareth? Did You come to destroy us? I know who You are—the Holy One of God!' But Jesus rebuked

*him, saying, 'Be quiet, and come out of him!' And when
the demon had thrown him in their midst, it came out of
him and did not hurt him. Then they were all amazed and
spoke among themselves, saying, 'What a word this is!
For with authority and power He commands the unclean
spirits, and they come out'".*

When a Church does not emphasize deliverance and
spiritual warfare, demons can find their way in and dwell there.
I have seen visitors attend Church services, even with titles like
Pastor, and by revelation discover that they were simply sent
by the devil to distract the Ministry. Some people with a Judas
spirit will operate as a spy or betrayer. It is critical for a Church
to pray for spiritual discernment.

Always be attentive to people joining a Church with spiritual titles. In 2010, while I was attending a conference in Atlanta,
Georgia (USA) with my wife, a woman came to visit our Church.
This woman introduced herself as *"Pastor"* and expressed a desire to our Church leaders about joining the Ministry. This was re-
ported to me upon my return. The following Sunday, this woman came to the front to receive prayer. The Lord revealed to me
that this woman, a visiting *"Pastor"*, was in fact a witch. My wife,
Pastor Anne, received the same revelation that day.

We decided to schedule a meeting with this woman pri-
vately on different day. I directly told her what the Lord told
me about her practice of witchcraft, and that she needed to
repent. She confirmed being involved in demonic, evil activ-
ity, and gave more details. She stated that her involvement in
witchcraft started in 2004, yet we knew it was much earlier. This
shows how the devil always tries to gain time by lying.

Certain circumstances helped us understand that this
woman's desire for deliverance was not sincere. To begin, she
came to our Church as *"Pastor"* while clearly knowing herself
that she was a witch. It was necessary for us to discern her involvement in witchcraft before she confessed it herself. We
were the first people to reveal this directly to her.

Since this woman was neither serious nor honest about the desire to be set free, we made the decision to not proceed with prayer for her deliverance. Admitting that deliverance is needed does not mean that a person is willing to go through it.

Honesty with God and oneself is essential for deliverance. A person needs to be truly sincere in his/her decision to walk in the light of Salvation, and whole-heartedly willing to be delivered. The Bible clearly shows that lying to the Holy Spirit brings grave consequences. In *Acts 5:1-9*, Ananias and his wife, Sapphira, agreed and lied to both the Holy Spirit and Apostle Peter. As a result, Ananias and his wife were both struck by God and died.

It is important to fear and honor the Lord, even though we live under His grace. Many Christians today take advantage of the grace of God, and sin even in the Church building. We find immature and unprepared leaders getting involved in conflict with people whom they are supposed to lead. The Church today needs to be cleaned and go back to holiness. Righteousness is the key for success, and the first attribute of the Kingdom of God. Outside of righteousness, it is impossible to dwell in the presence of the Lord. Many Churches are *"dead"* due to lack of righteousness and holiness.

Prayer and Fasting

In order to move God's people from the beginning step of Salvation into the Kingdom of God, the Church needs to put in place the conditions necessary for getting into the Kingdom of God. In other words, a deliverance department must be a part of the structure of each Church or group of Churches. This bridging yet critical step of deliverance is missing in many congregations in the Body of Christ today.

Deliverance is often missing because it requires prayer and fasting. Many people are not ready to make this sacrifice, or are distracted by food. In *Romans 14:17*, the Bible says, *"For the kingdom of God is not eating and drinking, but righteousness and peace and joy in the Holy Spirit"*. The Kingdom of God is accessible to a person who earnestly prepares himself/herself through three key elements for spiritual growth, which are meditation of the Word of God, prayer, and fasting.

Jesus Himself emphasized the significance of prayer and fasting, in addition to strong faith, in His instructions to the disciples about deliverance.

> "And Jesus rebuked the demon, and it came out of him; and the child was cured from that very hour. Then the disciples came to Jesus privately and said, 'Why could we not cast it out?' So Jesus said to them, 'Because of your unbelief; for assuredly, I say to you, if you have faith as a mustard seed, you will say to this mountain, 'Move from here to there,' and it will move; and nothing will be impossible for you. However, this kind does not go out except by prayer and fasting'". (Matthew 17:18-21)

Differing Views

Furthermore, deliverance is often missing in Churches because it is a controversial topic. Some Churches believe that a Christian can not be demon-possessed, whereas others believe that a Christian can be demon-possessed. Both opinions can be considered correct, depending on how a person defines being Christian.

- If Christian means being a Victorious believer, then Christians do not need deliverance.
- If Christian means being saved and does not include walking in daily Victory, then deliverance is needed.

This controversy can be addressed and resolved by defining the Kingdom of God, in addition to defining what it means to be Christian. If being saved equals being in Victory, then why did Jesus preach the Kingdom of God? Why did Jesus ask His disciples to wait for the coming of the Holy Spirit? (Acts 1:3-8)

The Kingdom of God is a platform in which Victorious Christians dwell and live. A Kingdom man/woman does not need deliverance, but instead he/she is filled and used by the Holy Spirit to operate deliverance. This is why Jesus asked His disciples to wait until they received the Holy Spirit in order to proceed and be efficient in the Kingdom of God.

Chapter 4
HOLY SPIRIT

Through water baptism, a person officially declares before Heaven and earth that he/she is serious about the decision of Salvation. John the Baptist led people to Salvation through repentance and water baptism, emphasizing the conditions required for Salvation through Jesus. John the Baptist's Ministry prepared the way for Jesus Christ. After accepting Jesus as Savior and being born again, the next transitional step is focused on the baptism in the Holy Spirit.

Two bodies of water

To better understand this step with the Holy Spirit, it is important to refer to the two bodies of water miraculously dried up by the Lord so that the people of Israel could move forward (Joshua 4:23). The first is the Red Sea, which typifies Salvation, and the second is the Jordan River, which symbolizes Victory and the Kingdom of God.

With each body of water, one side is wilderness. John the Baptist preached in the "wilderness", which refers to being saved yet outside the Kingdom of God (John 1:23-28). In the wilderness, people can not be stable and are nomads. In the wilderness, the dwelling tent is temporary. In the wilderness, you must fetch drinking water.

Before a person could cross the Jordan River, he/she needed to first move across the Red Sea from Egypt into the wilderness. Then, God's people crossed the Jordan River from the East to the West. "East" represents God's glory, from where our strength comes. "West" represents sunset and the final land to be conquered. Mature Christians move from East to West and enlarge their territory, while spiritually young Christians move from West to East and take refuge from the enemy on God's side. The direction of multiplication is always from East to West.

It is important to note that John the Baptist and Jesus ministered on both sides of the Jordan River. This represents the two steps to achieve the goal of helping people cross the Red Sea and Jordan River into Victory.

John the Baptist's Ministry emphasized repentance and Salvation. This saved people from danger, similar to how Moses led people out of Egypt from Pharaoh's oppression. John the Baptist was known as greater than any other Old Testament prophet because he finished up from where other prophets (including Moses) left off *(Luke 7:28)*. In other words, John the Baptist had the opportunity to make the connection between what was done previously and the emergence of Jesus' Ministry. He came to introduce Jesus and prepare the way.

Jesus' Ministry taught people how to move from the dry side to the wet, lush side of the Jordan River, which speaks about entering the Kingdom of God. In the Kingdom of God, every necessity is supplied from within, as everything that God's people needed was on the other side of the Jordan River. The action of crossing the Jordan River speaks about baptism in the Holy Spirit, as the action of crossing the Red Sea speaks about water baptism. This shows why water baptism occurs before baptism in the Holy Spirit, and establishes an order of occurrence.

The end of John the Baptist's era is illustrated by the conversion of water into wine by Jesus at the wedding at Cana in Galilee *(John 2:1-10)*. Water typifies Salvation and baptism, whereas wine represents the Holy Spirit. Jesus came to add the Holy Spirit to Salvation. These two steps (Salvation and the Holy Spirit) are key requirements for entry into the Kingdom of God. In other words, John the Baptist's teaching itself was not enough to get into the Kingdom of God. This explains why Jesus told His disciples to wait in Jerusalem until they received the Holy Spirit *(Acts 1:8)*.

For a person to move from Salvation into the Kingdom of God, he/she needs the baptism of the Holy Spirit. The baptism of the Holy Spirit is required in order to be operational in the Kingdom of God. For this reason, John the Baptist said, *"It is He who, coming after me, is preferred before me, whose sandal strap I am not worthy to loose" (John 1:27).* This verse demonstrates how the system shifted from water baptism into Holy Spirit baptism, and reveals the premise for establishing of the Kingdom of God.

Conditions for the Holy Spirit to dwell

The Holy Spirit can only be comfortable and fill a person if the spiritual transformation process has been triggered. The conditions necessary for the indwelling of the Holy Spirit are met after a person is both saved and born again. As described in previous sections of this book, the born again process includes different steps, including:

- Weakness identification and acknowledgement;
- Willingness to go through deliverance (if needed);
- Completion of deliverance;
- Becoming easy to work with;
- Progress in meditation of the Word of God, prayer, and fasting time.

If nothing is done to meet the conditions noted above, we should not expect the Holy Spirit to dwell in a person. The Holy Spirit can not dwell in sin, as revealed in *Isaiah 59:1-2.*

"Behold, the LORD's hand is not shortened, that it cannot save; nor His ear heavy, that it cannot hear. But your iniquities have separated you from your God; and your sins have hidden His face from you, so that He will not hear".

Furthermore, the Bible clearly says, *"For what fellowship has righteousness with lawlessness?" (2 Corinthians 6:14).* The Holy Spirit and sin are opposed. The Holy Spirit will never fellowship with sin. For the Holy Spirit to dwell in a person, he/she needs to renounce sin, and move toward holiness and righteousness.

In speaking about the Holy Spirit, Apostle Paul teaches that our body is designed to be the dwelling place of God's presence. The Bible says,

"Do you not know that your body is the temple of the Holy Spirit who is in you, whom you have from God, and you are not your own?" (1 Corinthians 6:19)

When a person allows the Holy Spirit to dwell and freely operate in himself/herself, this enables the *"tripod"* principle to be effectively applied. A tripod represents stability, which is necessary for progress in a person's spiritual life. The three tripod elements are:

· Word of God,
· Prayer, and
· Fasting.

The integration of these elements occurs through the Holy Spirit.

Using the Holy Spirit

The manifestation of the Holy Spirit in a person's life is introduced through baptism in the Holy Spirit *(Acts 2:1-4)*. The Holy Spirit comes with spiritual fire and empowers believers with different kinds of gifts *(1 Corinthians 12:4-11)*.

It is important to realize that many Churches believe in the Holy Spirit, but do not use it. The result, in this case, is similar to not believing. The main reason that the Holy Spirit was sent is to be used. In other words, *"If you don't use it, you lose it"*. Some people believe in the Holy Spirit but only use it in extreme cases, when sometimes it is already too late. In this way, the Holy Spirit has been applied like a suit worn only for special occasions, such as a wedding.

It is difficult to comprehend the message of the Kingdom of God without believing and being filled by the Holy Spirit. For this reason, Nicodemus did not understand when Jesus said a person must be born of water and Spirit in order to enter the Kingdom of God *(John 3:5)*.

In conclusion and before proceeding to the next chapter, it is important to note the pre-requisites for entry into the Kingdom of God: Repentance, Salvation, Born Again, and the Holy Spirit.

Chapter 5
KINGDOM OF GOD

Jesus introduced the Kingdom of God through His Ministry. His whole message was about the Kingdom of God. Even when Jesus sent His disciples, He directed them to cast out demons, heal the sick, and preach the Kingdom of God (Luke 9:1-2). Today, there is a lot of literature about the Kingdom of God, but very little is known about how to get in.

This chapter will help you address some key questions, including:

- What the Kingdom of God means;
- Why it is important to be in the Kingdom of God;
- When the Kingdom of God is going to happen;
- How to get in the Kingdom of God; and
- What are the attributes and benefits of the Kingdom of God?

What the Kingdom of God means

On earth, there are two main kingdoms. These are the Kingdom of God and the kingdom of devil, which is also called the "world".

The "world" is known to be a place where people worry, get oppressed and depressed, and then lose hope. In the world today, we find division between countries, communities, families, neighbors, and co-workers. The world has failed to solve the struggle and crisis of humanity. In this world today, no one has the answer—neither the people in positions to make decisions, nor those who are expected to follow them.

In contrast, the Kingdom of God is the system set by God to prevent faithful Believers from being subjected to the failure of the world. God intends for His children to live and dwell in righteousness, peace, and joy, three qualities that distinctly characterize the Kingdom of God *(Romans 14:17)*.

Why it is important to be in the Kingdom of God

Today, if you tell a person that you are Christian, he/she may not be surprised. However, if you tell a person that you do not worry, he/she would likely be in awe and impressed. Although knowing that Salvation provides a better life later in Heaven is important, people really need to know and live in Victory today.

To further understand the importance of being inside the Kingdom of God, let us refer back to an illustration from the Introduction of this book. You will agree with me that it is one thing to be alive, yet another to be in good health. Salvation keeps you alive, and the Kingdom of God keeps you in good health and Victory. The Kingdom of God relates to your spiritual health.

It is critical for all Christians to obtain the necessary teaching and revelation to live in Victory, in the Kingdom of God, every day.

When the Kingdom of God is going to happen

Many people, including Christians, have questions about the Kingdom of God just like Nicodemus. Jesus replied to Nicodemus' inquiry about how to get into the Kingdom of God, revealing that Salvation must come first. Jesus said, *"Unless one is born of water and the Spirit, he cannot enter the kingdom of God" (John 3:5)*. This implies that a person is saved and born again before entering the Kingdom of God.

Later on, the disciples asked Jesus why He spoke in parables with some people *(Matthew 13:10; Mark 4:11)*. An in-depth study of Jesus' answer confirms the sequence order from Salvation to the Kingdom of God. Jesus spoke to the *"outsiders"* in parables since the priority for them was not yet the Kingdom of God, but rather first to accept Jesus and be saved. However, Jesus spoke directly to His disciples since they were already saved, and therefore could understand the *"Kingdom"* language. In other words, a person can not comprehend the Kingdom of God if he/she is not yet saved.

How to get in the Kingdom of God

We previously discussed the steps to the Kingdom of God, which are Repentance, Salvation, Born Again, and the Holy Spirit. This successive order of these pre-requisites is important.

The Holy Spirit, being the last step prior to entry into the Kingdom of God, is highlighted in Jesus' statement, *"From the days of John the Baptist until now the kingdom of heaven suffers violence, and the violent take it by force"* (Matthew 11:12).

This *"force"* is related to the Holy Spirit, which is power, by definition. The similarity between power and Holy Spirit is illustrated when Jesus said, *"But you shall receive power when the Holy Spirit has come upon you..."* (Acts 1:8).

The Holy Spirit operates in both the physical and invisible realm. Therefore, the manifestation of the Holy Spirit is not necessarily something physical or tangible. At times we can perceive it, while at other times God purposely decides not to show it to us. For example, praying louder does not make a person's prayer more efficient. It is faith behind the prayer that makes the difference.

As a result, the *"force"* referred to by Jesus in *Matthew 11:12* is related to power coming from the Holy Spirit. In other words, entering the Kingdom of God is not about physical force, but rather a spiritual force which is generated by the Holy Spirit. Our prayer needs to be led by the Holy Spirit. This means, for example, that our prayer may be quiet at times and then louder at other times.

The Holy Spirit is the last step that a person must reach before getting into the Kingdom of God. A person can not operate in the Kingdom of God without the Holy Spirit.

What are the attributes and benefits of the Kingdom of God?

The fruit of the Kingdom of God is righteousness, whereas the fruit from following the "world" is sin. The outcome of righteousness is peace and joy, whereas the consequences of sin are worry, fear, anxiety, oppression, depression, and so on. To highlight the contrast between the Kingdom of God and the "world", Jesus said, "...If anyone loves the world, the love of the Father is not in him" (1 John 2:15).

The Bible clearly explains that the thinking of the flesh, which is sense and reason without the Holy Spirit, yields to misery from sin (Romans 8:6). A list of certain sins practiced in the "world" is found in Galatians 5:19-21.

> "Adultery, fornication, uncleanness, lewdness, idolatry, sorcery, hatred, contentions, jealousies, outbursts of wrath, selfish ambitions, dissensions, heresies, envy, murders, drunkenness, revelries, and the like...those who practice such things will not inherit the kingdom of God".

In the same chapter, the Bible clearly presents the fruit of the Holy Spirit, which characterizes the Kingdom of God.

> "But the fruit of the Spirit is love, joy, peace, longsuffering, kindness, goodness, faithfulness, gentleness, self-control" (Galatians 5:22-23).

Although the contrast between the Kingdom of God and the "world" is distinct, there are many Christians who are not completely free from the world's attributes. These Christians can be called "worldly Christians". In addition, there is another group of Christians who hate sin, but are missing the attributes of the Kingdom of God. These people lack teaching about the

Kingdom of God and the Holy Spirit. Jesus referred to this matter by saying, *"My people are destroyed for lack of knowledge"* (Hosea 4:6).

A key component of the Kingdom of God, righteousness, can be defined as right standing with God, with man, and with God's command. Righteousness yields to peace. Then, peace creates the condition for a person to be in joy. This peace refers to freedom from the devil, and does not rely on the absence of war. Jesus made a clear distinction between peace coming from Him, and what the world can offer *(John 14:27)*.

Righteousness sets a person free, whereas sin makes a person dependent on the devil, the accuser *(Revelation 12:10)*. In other words, living in holiness creates a platform for peace so that God can freely re-design a person's life according to His original plan in *Genesis 1:28*. God only operates in quietness and outside of agitation. This is supported by the fact that God put Adam asleep to create Eve. God did not need Adam's input to bless him. God's re-design process is called spiritual restoration. The end result of this restoration yields to joy. A person moves from the state of peace into the stage of blessings.

The goal of this book, as mentioned earlier, is to unfold the mystery about the Kingdom of God and to help people to move from the beginning step of being saved, to the step of walking in daily Victory.

Chapter 6
MANDATE

The next step after being faithful and efficient as a *"Kingdom man/woman"* is to receive a mandate to operate on God's behalf. It is important to clarify that having a mandate does not mean a person is called to Ministry, and furthermore that being called to Ministry does not give someone a mandate.

Power and authority

A mandate given by God incorporates two elements, power and authority. Power and authority are by definition different concepts and both necessary to function effectively at the mandate level.

Power is related to the ability or strength necessary to accomplish a task or execute an order. Power enables a person to comply with the authority. It is important to note that a person can have power without authority.

Authority is the legal right to apply power. Authority is the right to give orders. Authority and power are both needed to support each other and can reciprocally be undermined if one is lacking.

The example of a police officer can be used to demonstrate the working of power and authority. A police officer carries both power and authority. Power is represented by his gun, which can cause another person to stop. Authority is represented by his official badge, which authorizes the use of power.

Related to this example, we have judges. A judge has authority to enforce that laws are obeyed, but not power. Judges rely on the police to apply power. A judge's judgment from the authority can be executed with the police's power.

Due to the modernization of society, both power and authority have been misinterpreted. The example of a police officer is the perfect illustration. Today, we find some police officers abusing their power and authority, as well as some people refusing to submit to the authorities.

Another illustration of confusion with power and authority is seen with the concept of democracy. There are conflicts among the executive, legislative, and judiciary powers. Sometimes, it is not clear as to who really has the authority.

Similar to how a police officer has authority to lock or unlock according to the law, spiritual authority is given to Christians. The concept of authority and power is borrowed from the spiritual realm, yet has been altered by the modernization of society. The authority and power given by God to human kind relates directly to the spiritual level of mandate. In speaking to His disciples, Jesus explained,

> *"Behold! I have given you authority and power to trample upon serpents and scorpions, and physical and mental strength and ability over all the power that the enemy possesses; and nothing shall in any way harm you". (Luke 10:19; Amplified)*

Note here that Christians have received both authority and power, while the devil only has power. Everything that does not have God's approval is illegal. In order to effectively use this spiritual authority, a person must be living in righteousness. The devil does not have any legal right or authority to operate in a Christian's life, unless a door is opened by sin. This is why God's permission was required before the devil could touch Job's life (*Job 1:8-12*).

The Scripture is clear regarding the difference between authority and power. In *Revelation 12:10*, the Bible shows that Salvation precedes power, which precedes the Kingdom of

God, and then authority is the supreme. In other words, Salvation < Power < Kingdom of our God < Authority of His Christ.

The Key

The authority and power given to Christians by Jesus is symbolized by the key. A key regulates access and allows people to move from one side to another. A key is the operative tool proving the mandate or right given to a person to function on God's behalf.

The significance of the key is found in both the Old and New Testaments. The Old Testament *(Isaiah 22:22)* talks about the key given to Jesus, whereas the New Testament *(Matthew 16:19)* talks about the key transferred to Christians by Jesus through a person's entry in the Kingdom of God.

> *"The key of the house of David I will lay on his shoulder; so he shall open, and no one shall shut; and he shall shut, and no one shall open" (Isaiah 22:22).*

> *"I will give you the keys of the kingdom of heaven; and whatever you bind (declare to be improper and unlawful) on earth must be what is already bound in heaven; and whatever you loose (declare lawful) on earth must be what is already loosed in heaven" (Matthew 16:19; Amplified).*

In other words, Jesus transferred the authority and power given to Him by God the Father to Christians. It is interesting to note that these previous two Scriptures were fulfilled after John the Baptist perceived the key upon Jesus' shoulder and said, *"I need to be baptized by You, and are You coming to me?"* *(Matthew 3:14)*

The Kingdom of God, the fourth step, enables a person to get the key. Many people stop at the fourth step. In other words, they know the importance of the key, but they do not use it.

The fifth step, which is the mandate, enables a person to use it without always relying on the One who gave the key. This step which involves using the key requires spiritual training and perseverance. One thing is to get the key; another thing is to use it.

Qualified to Operate on God's Behalf

Jesus emphasizes the importance of receiving the necessary qualifications to operate on His behalf. For example, Jesus asked His disciples to wait in Jerusalem for the Holy Spirit before going to Judea, Samaria, and throughout the earth (Acts 1:8). Jesus' ultimate goal has always been for Christians to represent Him on earth. Jesus clearly said we will do more than demonstrated during His Ministry on earth.

> "Most assuredly, I say to you, he who believes in Me, the works that I do he will do also; and greater works than these he will do, because I go to My Father" (John 14:12).

This verse does not imply that Christians will be more powerful than Jesus. The miracles performed by Jesus can be considered a display model. What a person sees in a display window before entering a store is actually less than contained in the store. Victorious Christians will follow the model of Jesus, and do more.

Elijah and Moses

In the Bible, the Prophet Elijah was a "Kingdom man" with a mandate to operate on God's behalf. In response to the rebellion of king Ahab against God, which was more extreme than any previous king, Elijah declared a drought.

> "As the LORD God of Israel lives, before whom I stand, there shall not be dew nor rain these years, except at my word" (1 Kings 17:1).

Elijah did not say, "God told me", but rather he commanded, "Except at my word". The point was not to go to God for directions, but rather to operate on God's behalf. When you

have received the key, you do not need to go back to the One who gave it to you. This key transfer occurs in the last step, just as when a person buys a house the keys are handed over after all administrative paperwork is done.

In the example of Elijah, he demonstrated Victorious behavior by standing against king Ahab and acting on God's behalf. We can see God's approval in His response to Elijah's Kingdom behavior. God agreed with Elijah's declaration by directing him to safety away from the drought, hiding by the Brook Cherith, which leads into the Jordan River (*1 Kings 17:2-7*).

Elijah's approach is different than Moses' behavior. Elijah made decisions according to the mandate received from the Lord. Moses went back and forth from the mountain to receive instructions from God, and then transferred a message to God's people. Today, Moses would be the perfect example of a *"mailman"*. Moses was a Salvation man, whereas Elijah was a Kingdom man.

One illustration of Elijah leading Moses can be found in *Mark 9:2-9*. When Jesus was transfigured in the sight of His disciples, the Bible says that Elijah appeared *"accompanied"* by Moses. Peter was amazed in seeing the glory of God upon Jesus, and even asked to dwell longer there with Him. We can only experience this glory and Victory of God if we ourselves go through the process of transfiguration, in which our old self shifts into a new nature. This is called going to the next level in our spiritual life. The fact that Elijah was *"accompanied"* by Moses shows that someone having the mandate (Elijah) comes with the foundation of Salvation (Moses), but Salvation itself is not enough to walk in daily Victory. The importance of mandate is emphasized.

God is looking for people who are available to be used on His behalf. We are not being called to quit, but to win. The ultimate goal is to operate on God's behalf. This means using the key that has been given to us.

DISCUSSION

The importance of moving from Salvation into the Kingdom of God is something that I can speak of personally. My wife and I were born in Ivory Coast (West Africa), and later moved to Belgium (Europe) to study for eight years. My wife studied Accounting, and I studied Microbiology. After completing my PhD, we moved to the USA. Ever since being married, we had desired to have a child. We tried all kinds of medical substances. At that time, I did not really know about the Kingdom of God. The kind of teaching that I had received was wrong because it assimilated the Kingdom of God to Heaven. The difference between the Kingdom of God and Heaven was not clear in my mind. In other words, I was saved but not a Victorious Christian.

One day in our Church, a prophet came as a guest speaker from the state of Florida. He prophesied that my wife and I would have a child, and that my wife would be pregnant in six months. The prophecy occurred in January. In April of the same year we moved from the state of Vermont to Minnesota. Before moving, my wife was taking fertility medication. After moving, some of our items remained in boxes, including the medication. We had forgotten about the prophecy, even though we had been very excited when we received it. Then, in June, my wife became pregnant without any fertility medication.

God demonstrated that nothing is impossible for Him, and He can even make rivers in the wilderness *(Isaiah 43:18-19)*. Sometimes when we try to compete with or help God in our blessing, God can purposely delay things until we come to the conclusion that He does not need our help to bless us. In the circumstance with my wife and I, God showed that He did not need medication to do what was prophesied six months prior. This event was the beginning of a long and wonderful journey with God.

During my wife's eighth month of pregnancy, we went to the hospital due to some pain. The medical exams revealed a serious situation. Before further examination, they asked us to complete and sign a form. The hospital wanted to decline responsibility for any results, because my wife or my baby's life could be taken away. At that time, I heard the devil trying to speak, intimidate, and laugh at me. I knew that it was not the physician speaking, but the devil was trying to impress me with lies. I became nervous, and even started crying inside. I was not spiritually strong enough to fight against the devil's manipulation and intimidation. This shows the importance of being a Victorious Christian.

After I signed the form, I decided to drive all the way home as quickly as possible in order to call two people overseas. After driving thirty minutes, I first called my mother, who was a deacon in Ivory Coast at her Church. I had emotion in my voice and remember her asking if I was crying. I answered, "Yes, Mom", and explained the situation. She comforted me by saying, "Do not cry, I'm going to pray the whole night and Jesus will solve it". Next, I called my friend from our former Church in Belgium. I was bothered to wake both my mom and friend up in the middle of the night. It was 6 PM in Minnesota, midnight in Ivory Coast, and 1 AM in Belgium. After the phone calls, both people agreed to pray for us until they received any updates.

On my way returning to the hospital, the Lord started speaking to me, and asked this question: "Do you really need to drive all the way home to ask someone to pray for you? How long have you been Christian? Why are you not able to pray? Why are you running like a 'chicken'? Why are you afraid?"

I started crying even more, and I realized that something was missing in my Christian life. I realized that all of God's promises were not fulfilled in my life. I realized that I needed to do something more. I realized that I needed to be more aggressive. Something was starting to build inside of me. The more I cried, the more I was upset against the devil. It came to my mind that if those two people can pray (in Ivory Coast and Belgium), then I can do the same and pray.

To conclude this testimony, my wife and I returned home from the hospital the next day. She was healed and the pain went away. Amen. My daughter was born the next month. Everything was fine with both my wife and daughter. Our daughter is a part of the Ministry and travels with us in serving the Lord.

At that point, my spiritual life changed dramatically. I decided to do something. I decided to fast and pray more, to spend more time in the Bible, and to seek understanding. This was a turning point in my spiritual life. Today, the devil can not do such things to us. We now play "offense" and no longer "defense". In other words, we do not wait until the devil attacks before we react. We are "proactive". To God be all the glory!!

Many Christians are in the kind of situation that I just explained. They are saved, yet they can not fight for themselves, and can not fight for their family. They are Christian, yet defeated by the devil.

To better illustrate situations like this testimony in relation to the five spiritual levels, I will summarize certain characteristics at each level. This can be seen in **Table 4**.

Table 4. Examples of some Attributes at each step

	Before	After
Salvation	• Addiction • Blood line • Confusion • Discouragement • Doubt & Negativity • Fear & Worry • Unforgiveness	Same as before Salvation
Born Again	Same as before Salvation	• Weakness identified • Willing to go through deliverance • Deliverance completed • Prayer & Fasting life • Easy to work with • Regular at church • Faithful in Tithe
Holy Spirit	Same as after Born Again	• Not afraid • Do not complain • Thirsty for God • Gift of Holy Spirit • Can pray for others • Can do deliverance
Kingdom of God	Same as after Holy Spirit	• Righteousness • Peace & Joy • Love & Faithfulness • Gentleness • Goodness &Kindness • Self-Control
Mandate	Same as after Kingdom of God	• Walking in Authority • Dominion

As mentioned previously, Salvation is for Heaven. The decision to give our life to God does not mean that our life on earth has already changed. Salvation does not automatically make a person's behavior different.

Being born again is the fruit resulting from Salvation, our Heavenly citizenship. The process of mind renewal is a part of being born again. At this step, the mind is set on Heaven and some attributes can be seen, such as prayer, fasting, willingness to go through deliverance, and faithfulness in tithes.

Our relationship with God is firmly established in the born again step. God can only fellowship with us when sin is no longer between us. In other words, Salvation corresponds to a man who is engaged with a woman, whereas being born again equals someone who is married with a woman. Salvation speaks of willingness to walk with Jesus, whereas being born again refers to action. Being born again is a critical step.

At the next step, we must note that the Holy Spirit can not dwell with fear. Additionally, when a person operates in the Holy Spirit, he/she can pray for others.

Next, when a person is in the Kingdom of God, it is not only worry that is gone. This person will also manifest certain attributes, such as peace, joy, kindness, goodness, love, gentleness, self-control.

The last step is receiving the mandate to operate on God's behalf. You walk in authority and dominion. A Kingdom man/woman can convert dry land into something wet at any time. This explains why Abraham let his nephew, Lot, pick land first. A Kingdom man/woman has the privilege to receive and interpret important information from God. For example, Daniel and Joseph were both able to interpret dreams. Furthermore, a Kingdom man/woman can command things to happen. For this purpose, God told Joshua that he possessed the area where his feet tread.

Where do you position yourself?

Through your reading of this book, I would like to ask you, *"Where do you position yourself in Table 4?"*

As when reading a map, it is important to position yourself in order to determine your direction. This will enable you to lay down a strategy to improve your spiritual life.

Righteousness is a pivotal element for success and change in your spiritual life. God pays respect and takes into account the point of view of a righteous person. When God was about to destroy Sodom and Gomorrah, God let Abraham know and did not violate the authority He had given to Abraham. Furthermore, Abraham negotiated with God until his nephew, Lot, was saved.

Today, the percentage of Christians living in Victory is small. The majority are saved but living in defeat and fear of the enemy. We find Christians who worry, can not fight and pray for their own healing, and can not pray for others. We find Christians who complain and murmur every day, and walk according to a mood that changes like the weather. These are Christians who have crossed the *"Red Sea"* but are still in the *"wilderness"*. They have not yet crossed the *"Jordan River"* to enter the *"Promise Land"*. They are stuck somewhere, like Israel was stuck for 40 years.

We are preaching the Gospel to help Christians move from the beginning step of being saved into living in Victory every day. God is looking for Christians who are living in Victory, which means living in the Kingdom of God.

Staying in the Kingdom of God requires your input and spiritual hard work. Contrarily, there are two ways of being lazy: either not working at all on your spiritual life, or working hard but inefficiently. Hearing and applying the message of the Kingdom of God boosts your efficiency and helps you to understand, comprehend and walk by revelation. When you walk in the Kingdom of God, you walk in righteousness. A Kingdom man/woman does not worry and can not be intimidated. The devil can not impress a Kingdom man/woman, and therefore the devil is not going to waste time trying.

Often times when presenting Jesus to people, the response is *"I already have my Church"*. The point is not to have a Church, but the point is to live in Victory. Some Churches emphasize Salvation like the ultimate goal, yet it is actually the beginning. We have to push to get to the end, which is better.

Some Churches believe in the Holy Spirit, and some do not. Some Churches believe in the Holy Spirit but do not use it. Some Churches believe in the Holy Spirit and use it.

Where do you locate your congregation?

Figure 1 provides an overview of different groups of congregations in the Body of Christ. A point of common ground we all share is that Salvation comes only through faith in Jesus Christ. There are basically four different groups of Churches.

- Congregations not aware or believing in the Holy Spirit;
- Congregations not believing in the manifestation of the Holy Spirit;
- Congregations assimilating the Kingdom of God to Heaven; and
- Congregations having knowledge of and preaching the Kingdom of God.

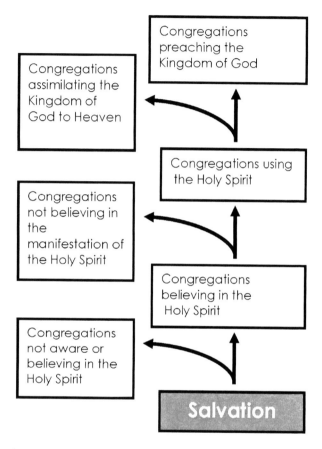

Figure 1. Overview of Different Groups of Congregations in the Body of Christ

To further understand the Kingdom of God in regards to your congregation and spiritual life, we can study the significance of certain men of God alongside each of the five spiritual levels. The Bible gives us examples typifying the different steps.

Table 5 provides a map of input and results with each step, and key people. Note that among the list of men of God in this Table 5, two of them (Elijah accompanied by Moses) appeared with Jesus on the mountain during the transfiguration. The chronological order from Moses to the Apostles (with the exception of Elijah) follows the successive order of the five spiritual steps from Salvation to Mandate. Each step is important for our spiritual life.

Table 5. Example of Man of God and type of Ministry in relation with the five steps

Input	Results	Man of God
Salvation	Citizen of Heaven	Moses (Exodus 11:1-3)
Repentance	Born Again	John the Baptist (Matthew 3:1-2)
Holy Spirit	Operating in the Holy Spirit	The Apostles (Acts 2:1-4)
Kingdom of God	Victory	The Apostles (Acts 8:12)
Mandate	Jesus' Ambassador	Elijah (1 Kings 17:1-5)
		The Apostles (Mark 6:7)*

*Reference from Amplified Bible
"And He called to Him the Twelve [apostles] and began to send them out [as His ambassadors] two by two and gave them authority and power over the unclean spirits" (Mark 6:7)

To visualize the change and growth with each of the five steps, **Figure 2** incorporates the seed development cycle. Every Christian should go through the five different steps.

The first generation seed represents Jesus crucified and put in the ground for three days. Through Jesus' resurrection we receive Salvation, and through seed germination we are given a new nature. In other words, our flesh gets crucified and we are born again by abandoning our old and sinful nature.

The Holy Spirit, which is represented by the tree, then grows in us and His manifestation becomes more and more obvious. The Holy Spirit is a high priority for God, as the tree of life was in the center of the garden. The fruit coming out of the Holy Spirit, symbolized by righteousness, peace, and joy, appears at this level. This step is called the Kingdom of God.

The last step is the appearance and spreading of the second generation seed, which symbolizes the mandate given to a Kingdom man/woman to operate on God's behalf. One seed from the first generation yields to several seeds at the second generation. At this step, the blessing pronounced by God in *Genesis 1:28* is manifested. Jesus' presence in us enables one seed to multiply and generate many fruit, each with several seeds in them. This law of multiplication was established by God in *Genesis 1:11*.

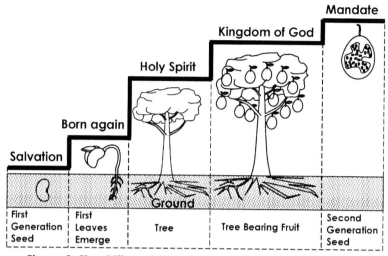

Figure 2. Five Different Steps Toward Victory

God's ultimate goal is to move us from being the ground to being the second generation seed. This process can only be possible if the first generation seed, Jesus Christ, is allowed to be sown in the ground and go through the process of bearing fruit. Jesus called us to be disciples, not only Christian. When someone is saved yet has not taken additional steps, he/she needs assistance. When a person has a mandate, he/she gives assistance to others. The Bible says that it is more blessed to give than receive. We have been called to assist other people, to serve the Lord, and to be efficient.

CONCLUSION

My goal in this book has been to give you key teaching to highlight the urgency of moving from the state of being saved to the state of walking in daily Victory. It is time to be busy with God's business. It is time to press in. The Body of Christ needs to understand that it is time to preach the Kingdom message. It is time to emphasize the importance of being a Victorious Christian. It is time to upgrade the system.

We are living in a time where there is more and more oppression, and more and more depression. Today, it takes more than just *"I believe"* or *"Hallelujah"*. What was wrong yesterday is right today; what was right yesterday is wrong today. The system is simply upside down. We have conflict between parents and children, conflict between teachers and students, and conflict between managers and workers. Pressure is everywhere. The *"world"* system has failed to solve the humanity crisis. It is time to turn to God. It is time to get into the Kingdom of God. It is time to walk in daily Victory. We refuse to be defeated Christians. We refuse to be broke financially. We refuse to be sick. We refuse to struggle. For we have been called to walk in Victory.

God is working at two levels:

· God is creating a new generation of Christians with a Kingdom mind-set. This new generation reminds us of Joshua and Caleb.
· God is re-orienting Pastors and Christian leaders from the old system to preach the Kingdom message.

Both groups are merging into one point, which is the Kingdom of God. In *Luke 16:16*, the Bible talks about the urgency of pressing into the Kingdom of God. It took 2000 years for Christians to understand the concept of the Kingdom of God. Today, it is about the Kingdom of God because we are living in the end times. It is the same kind of situation that the disciples were facing at the beginning of the Church. We are feeling the same kind of pressure that the Church was facing in the book of *Acts*. In all types of processes, the beginning and end are key elements, because both refer to a gate. Either closing or opening the gate requires force. New challenge requires a new approach to overcome it. This is why the term *"Apostle"* has been reintroduced. The end times are dealing with the same gate that the first generation Apostles opened. The same *"spiritual turbulence"* that defeated the devil by establishing Jesus' Church in the book of *Acts* with the Apostles is now back to close the deal before the rapture. In other words, God is putting in place the same system that defeated the devil 2000 years ago. Every new move begins in the womb of the old.

YOUR ROLE IN ADVANCING GOD'S KINGDOM

Dear friend,

Thank you for reading this book and sharing our vision, which is to help God's people move from the beginning step of Salvation to walking daily in the Kingdom of God. This vision of Heaven Citizenship Ministries has sent us to different nations in Europe, Africa, Asia, and America. God has given us a specific mandate to expand the Kingdom of God in all nations, as well as to empower and teach Christians to live in Victory. One part of the vision is helping those called to Ministry to obtain the necessary training to preach the Kingdom message. We interact with local Pastors around the world to bring revival. God is touching and renewing the hearts and minds of His people, and bringing them to the next step. Thank you for your role in advancing God's Kingdom.

God bless you,

Apostle Francois Ahimou

Expanding the Kingdom of God in all Nations

For more information, please visit our website:

www.heavencitizenship.org

or contact us:

Heaven Citizenship Ministries

P.O. Box 65852

Saint Paul, Minnesota 55165
(USA)

Phone:

651-274-3244

Email:

info@heavencitizenship.org